"Richard La Motte loves his craft and it shows in every line. He has given us a comprehensive, step-by-step analysis of the costume designer's work. The book is of great value to both the interested amateur and the budding professional."

> **—John Bloomfield**
> Costume Designer: *The Mummy,*
> *Waterworld, Scorpion King*

"This book should become the bible for other costume designers. It's clear and comprehensive."

> **—Erica Phillips**
> Costume Designer: *The Perfect Storm,*
> *Air Force One, The General's Daughter,*
> *Outbreak*

"An accurate and insightful look at the behind-the-scenes requirements for anyone interested in a career in Wardrobe... an entertaining read for the general public as well as professionals."

> **—Molly Harris Campbell**
> Costume Designer: *Beverly Hills 90210,*
> *The X-Files*

"It unlocks the door to costume design in a way that makes complex concepts easy to understand... I wish I had a book like this when I was starting out."

> **—Robert Turturice**
> Costume Designer: *Batman and Robin,*
> *The Flintstones in Viva Rock Vegas*

"Learning about motion picture costuming, when I began my career thirty some years ago, was largely a matter of luck. Hopefully you'd find a good mentor and not make too many mistakes. Richard La Motte's book on costuming and costume design should be required reading for anyone contemplating this sort of career. It leads you through the various aspects of costuming in easy-to-understand language and is obviously written by a person with *real* experience and a true passion for his work."

> **—Donna Roberts**
> Vice President
> Western Costume Company

MICHAEL WIESE PRODUCTIONS
www.mwp.com

Since 1981, Michael Wiese Productions has been dedicated to providing novice and seasoned filmmakers with vital information on all aspects of filmmaking and videomaking. We have published more than 50 books, used in over 500 film schools worldwide.

Our authors are successful industry professionals — they believe that the more knowledge and experience they share with others, the more high-quality films will be made. That's why they spend countless hours writing about the hard stuff: budgeting, financing, directing, marketing, and distribution. Many of our authors, including myself, are often invited to conduct filmmaking seminars around the world.

We truly hope that our publications, seminars, and consulting services will empower you to create enduring films that will last for generations to come.

We're here to help. Let us hear from you.

Sincerely,

Michael Wiese
Publisher, Filmmaker

COSTUME

DESIGN 101

The Art and Business of Costume Design
for Film and Television

by
Richard La Motte

Published by Michael Wiese Productions
11288 Ventura Blvd., Suite 821
Studio City, CA 91604
tel. (818) 379-8799
fax (818) 986-3408
mw@mwp.com
www.mwp.com

Cover Design: Alexander Arkadin
Cover Art: Richard La Motte
Book Layout: Gina Mansfield

Printed by McNaughton & Gunn, Inc., Saline, Michigan
Manufactured in the United States of America

ISBN 0-941188-35-3

Library of Congress Cataloging-in-Publication Data

La Motte, Richard E., 1943–
    Costume design 101: the art and business of costume design for film and television/ by Richard E. La Motte.
        p. cm.
    Includes bibliographical references.
    ISBN 0-941188-35-3
        1. Costume. 2. Costume design. I. Title: Costume design one hundred and one. II. Title.

PN1995.9.C56 D32 2001
791.43'026—dc21

2001035805
CIP

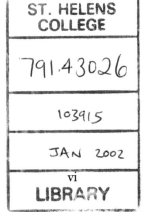

vi

TABLE OF CONTENTS

"Every film is a spiritual quest."

— Akira Kurosawa

ACKNOWLEDGMENTS

All life, to be in any way successful, has to be collaborative, and this means give and take. So far, I feel that I have taken far more than I have given.

I would like to remember and thank just a few of the many people who have helped me over the years.

Edith Head and Dorothy Jeakins, whose instruction and casual-looking attention to detail are still an inspiration.

Al Nickel and Lilly at old Western Costume who helped many a designer with their kindness and skill. I still remember showing a sketch to Al, Western's in-house designer, who had both a rich past history in theater and an accomplished art style. He reviewed my sketch and never betrayed a moment of doubt. "These are wonderful.... Lilly, come here." And she did. Lilly, Western's head cutter-fitter, looked at my very unaccomplished renderings. "Beautiful, darling, makes me want to cry a little." She wrapped a protective arm around me as she shepherded me toward the workroom. "Come on, darling, let's see what we can do."

Dick James, Wesley Trist, Ed Wynigear, the three old-timers at Fox who taught me how to prepare and execute shows and many other lessons of the wardrobe department.

Mike Butler, Pat Cummings, Diana Duran, Bob Labansat, Bud Clark, and all the other costumers I have done locations with over the years.

My mother, Lucy La Motte, herself a great cutter-fitter, who helped me get in the business and taught me so much about it and about life as well.

FOREWORD

I've tried to think of the best way to format this book so that it might be the most help to those who read it.

The publisher tells me that the biggest audience for this series of books on filmmaking are entry-level personnel, film students, and people new in the business who are trying to polish their skills.

With this in mind, I went to a book store and looked over the selection of books available on the costume department. What I found were books that explained period fashions, theatrical costume construction, and one book on "tips" for costumers. What I didn't find was a book that told you how to budget the wardrobe department for a film or TV show, how to break down a script for department requirements, how to understand the various concept styles of theatrical costume design, or how to run a department as a supervisor or designer — in other words, a book that gives you "real world" insights and information about a real job that you might actually be starting. Well, that's the book I've tried to write.

My experience is that, while many people feel that they are capable of, and have a desire to be theatrical costume designers, they don't realize that in order to be successful, they have to have a successful department behind them, one that is able to:

- **ONE** Handle the financial responsibilities of the department.

- **TWO** Be able to provide and maintain the costumes required.

- **THREE** Be able to work the clothes in front of the camera.

- **FOUR** Know how to wrap the department with no loose ends.

I have tried to separate the job requirements in their own chapters, chronologically... that is, in the order of how a show works from the time that you get a script; this means that a lot of information is repeated from various angles at different times in the process. But this way, anyone can look up any area or read the whole book for a comprehensive overview.

I have written from personal experience, and because personal experience can differ from one to another, there will be some who have found other ways of doing things. This is okay. I am a firm believer that the right way is the way that *works*.

The area of costume design is a great field in which to earn a living. I've had the opportunity to travel; meet interesting (and some famous) people; had the terrific satisfaction of seeing my decisions displayed on the big screen; and been paid to do it. For a lot of people, myself included, it doesn't get any better than that.

Costume design and department supervision aren't as daunting or over-whelming as they might be if you keep a few things in mind:

- People no smarter than you do it successfully.

- What you don't know, you can learn.

- It's all based on organization.

Also, I tend to repeat myself on some things, but that's because they are the things that warrant repeating.

I thought that I would start by introducing myself in order to share with you the progression of the jobs I've held, and through that, describe how the major studio costume departments were run, how we learned our jobs and what they were like.

Please don't be intimidated by the technical or financial sections on department budgets. When you need to know, it will all make sense.

INTRODUCTION

I don't know exactly when I got interested in the idea of costumes. It may have been during those childhood days watching epics like *Ben-Hur* and *Ulysses* or Westerns like *Shane* and being just blown away by the sheer scale of them, or the movies' ability to transport me into another world or time.

My first firsthand experience with a wardrobe department occurred when I was eleven years old and was hired by Paramount Pictures as an extra during summer vacation. The movie they were making was *The Ten Commandments*. I still have wonderful memories of C. B. De Mille in his riding breeches shouting through his handheld megaphone at the background people and encouraging us to make it believable. Being on the set with all those extras in costume and makeup was an exercise in the magic of make-believe that I never forgot.

My tenure in the biz owes as much to nepotism (in the grand Hollywood tradition) as anything else. My mother, Lucy, was a world-class cutter-fitter, that is, the union job description for the highest level of garment maker there is; she made dresses for ice shows, burlesque houses, stage reviews, personal sales, and the movies, including gowns worn in *Gone with the Wind*.

For years she worked with Edith Head, realizing in cloth what Edith created on paper. Of course, after growing up surrounded by seamstresses (some years the workroom at Paramount was my day care center) I developed an undying love for their skill and an inside appreciation of the problems of the workroom and costume manufacture.

I was fortunate enough to have a few other experiences that aimed me or armed me in my career choice. Growing up in West L.A. after WWII was one of them; in those days, television showed a lot of films from the thirties and forties; these are still among the best costumed shows ever filmed. Producers had a commitment to quality and they realized that if half of the films' attraction was the star and the story, the visual scale and artistry made up the other half. They went to great lengths to create periods, foreign settings and characters in movies that are still satisfying today; watching those films fired my imagination (and still does) with a desire to re-create history and to create characters through the medium of costumes.

Growing up in the fifties offered other unique circumstances; there were war surplus stores that sold militaria; and kids, myself included, bought, swapped, and sold war souvenirs. Sometimes when we'd play "army" in the dirt alleys or have dirt-clod fights in the vacant lots, we'd wear German helmets, carry Japanese rifles, festoon our grubby T-shirts with tank assault badges and iron crosses. Also, quite a few of my friends' fathers were veterans and I spent more than one night in quiet garages listening with rapt attention while getting a history lesson on the war, accompanied by a display of "neat stuff." My own father had been in WWI in the Royal Flying Corps, and gave me all his uniforms and flying gear (which I still have)... anyway, a love of uniforms has persisted.

The big influence, of course, was home. Mom used to bring home beautiful costumes to work on, and the house was full of costume books. All this made me want to draw... so I copied pictures out of war books, costume books, art books, *National Geographic*. Nothing teaches you what goes where like drawing it; you have to think of everything or it doesn't get in the picture. Luckily, my family always encouraged my drawing ability, and today, while not a great artist by any means, I can do solid, readable renderings.

I believe that every designer should be able to draw as a way of communicating ideas to coworkers. A few quick sketches in front of a director or production designer is truly worth a thousand words, and talking over a quick sketch or "cartoon" with the person who has to make the costume is a real necessity.

The final great career shaper was my stint in the Marine Corps. I joined after high school in the early sixties, and soon learned the meaning of the Marine motto, "Gung ho!", from the Chinese meaning "work together." The Corps taught me several applicable lessons, among them:

- No organization works without a clear chain of command.

- Leadership is most effective when done from the front.

- Planning is central to the success of any mission.

- Good morale is invaluable for sustaining team effort in the face of adversity.

- A unit's (department's) ability and flexibility in meeting the challenges of changing situations is reliant on the organization of its supplies.

- In all situations: determination, clear thinking and quick decision-making based on good information will be the deciding factors.

All these principles become very helpful when applied to filmmaking.

I got out of the Marine Corps in 1965 and went to work as an illustrator for a silk screen company that did prints for motel chains among other things. A few months later, Lucy told me about a studio apprenticeship program being offered by the Motion Picture Producers Association. I interviewed and was offered a position in the wardrobe department at Fox Studios.

About this time I was introduced to my wife, Patricia. My mother was working as the head of the women's workroom at CBS Studio Center, and her male counterpart, Bob Parral, was running the men's tailor shop, himself an excellent coat maker. They decided that his daughter, Patricia, should widen her circle of acquaintances and as I was just getting out of the service, well... We were married less than a year later, our union having been brokered in the workroom. Her younger sister, Loree Parral, also became a costumer, and has been nominated eleven times for Emmys for costumes, and won twice, for shows including *L.A. Law*, *Picket Fences*, and many others. She's really the pride of the family and regularly gets write-ups in papers and magazines for creating trend-setting "looks" for award-winning shows.

When I went to work at Fox it was during the last days of the "studio system" when studios made their own films and ran huge lot departments to facilitate them.

The wardrobe department occupied several buildings and storage spaces. My job as "stock clerk" or the "upstairs maid" as it was sometimes called, was: Keep these areas clean. Order the stock. Learn what all those cloths were (miles of them). Shine shoes and boots. Block and clean hats. Help costumers pull garments for their shows. Measure and size all returning stock.

Doing "returns" can be quite a learning experience. Returns occur when a project finishes shooting. (See Chapter 10, The Wrap, for details.) At that time, the costumes used are returned to their place of origin. Sometimes they have been packed with care, cleaned and sorted; sometimes, owing to time or other conditions, the clothes are returned dirty and unsorted.

Doing returns means going through the costume inventory of a show item by item looking for damages, while checking the items against the original billing sheets for losses; then breaking down (separating) the stock and sending out the cleaning; then, upon the cleaners' return, sizing (that is, measuring) the clothes, tagging them, and returning them to their place of storage, usually by period and type of garment.

Spending weeks or months doing this is very instructive. You can see how different costumers and designers use the same clothes in various combinations for different effects. How selection and overdying have developed various color schemes. How cleverly planned manufacture, dovetailed into existing stock, gives a "new" look. You can see costs related to repairable damages that could have been avoided, and most of all you learn to appreciate an organized return. Another benefit I derived from working in the department was the lunch time use of the Research Room. I would brown bag my lunch and spend at least an hour a day going through old show still books and historical clip files while I ate.

When I was starting out I had the good fortune to apprentice under an older costume department head named Dick James. He mentored me with humorous sternness. His advice was, "Rich, this is a wonderful business... you can do anything you want, travel, make good money, meet wonderful people... only two things you can't do: Never be late, never make a mistake." This proved to be true advice in every sense.

As the costumers developed some confidence in me, they would request that I assist them in "pulling" their shows. At Fox in the sixties, the senior costumers had been there since the thirties and had done such shows as *Viva Zapata* and *The Grapes of Wrath*, many times without designers. In those early days, designers usually came onto shows only when manufacture was expected, doing the dresses for the leading lady or changes for the male cast (except in the case of some musicals where everything was designed). Rarely did designers stick around for the whole show, as is the norm now. Pulling a show consisted of helping to assemble the costumes that would be used on a project under the direction of the costume supervisor, who had been assigned the show by the studio department head. These old guys were tough taskmasters, but knew more about wardrobe, periods, and the basic nuts and bolts of running a show than anybody else; it was an eye-opening training ground into the realities of production. They were masters at the art of film production and at anticipating the problems that would be a normal part of any film. Their forte was the creation of strong "character" wardrobe with its attendant jobs of aging and distressing. They were dedicated researchers who assessed every piece of wardrobe on its historical as well as artistic merits. Of course some were better at it than others, but one only has to watch the clothes in those films made from the twenties to the fifties (and many even later) to see how good they were. Oh yes, in those days nobody from Wardrobe got screen credit except designers and studio lot department heads.

My department progress followed the course of many. In my next job, I was fed out on lot shows as "day check help." These were valuable training days that occurred when television shows or feature films had large extra calls and needed additional wardrobe labor to help wrangle the background players. Whether on the lot or on a location, here is where we learned what a shooting show was about; I experienced the day-to-day logistical problems our department met in providing for the show's requirements. You generally had large crowds to dress and learned quick techniques for extras' fittings, which included: eyeballing a person's head-to-toe sizes; being able to talk your way through the concerns of balking extras and "keep the line moving"; quick repairs and alterations using needle and thread, fabric tape and iron, box stapler and/or two-faced tape; all this while checking the extras both in and out.

Controlling wardrobe stock at this job level is everything. Lack of attention to detail here results in losses to the ever-present souvenir hunters.

It wasn't long before I was sent on shows as a set costumer and had the opportunity to follow the show's progress from beginning to end (at the lowest level of responsibility). I would work with my counterparts in production, young second assistant directors, (some of whom have gone on to head studio production departments) in dovetailing production requirements with wardrobe department realities in terms of scheduling and the number of dressed bodies required in front of camera.

At this stage, among other things, we started to learn the magic of aging and distressing, long-held department secrets for breaking down costumes to give them the appearance of age. This job, sometimes done on a huge scale, made the difference between a "real" looking show and a "costume-y" one.

I then worked several shows as key set. That is, I handled all the clothing for the cast, readied their daily changes according to the call sheet, saw to it that they had their appropriate costumes on when they went before camera, and I was also in charge of keeping the set book. I worked closely with the script girl, developing all the matching information for continuity. Here is also where we learned to work closely with the camera folks — what were they seeing? Did the actor's shoes matter? Was the stain on the pants or dress in the shot? Only the camera operator knows for sure. The key set job is the most important job in the department with regard to day-to-day set operations; and when the shooting day is over, it's the set person who retrieves the costumes, returns them to the department, separates and sends out the cleaning, then checks to make sure all is ready for tomorrow's work.

Eventually the department decided that I was ready for a show of my own and allowed me to supervise a television pilot. Now I could bring to bear everything I had learned with the addition of new responsibilities: breaking down the script for costume department requirements, researching periods and searching out where these costumes were, if they were there at all, for my meetings with the producer, unit manager (now called line producer), and for my concept meetings with the director — which would begin a process of collaboration that would involve actors, extras, and every other department represented on the shoot.

As supervisor I was still expected to "pull" my own show and if I had help I was to give them direction. In other words, I started to learn how to assemble a department with both material and personnel.

The biggest new challenge involved actors; up to this time I had worked with actors on the set but had never before helped select what costumes they would wear, nor had I ever helped them get fitted by the tailor shop and then get costumes approved by the director before being used in the film. Now I found that while all my technical knowledge was necessary to get the show done at the physical level, I needed to be able to think in other areas — areas that were conceptual, artistic, that had to do more with psychology, timing, and ego than with costumes.

I realized that if I wanted to be able to influence what was worn, and not just take orders to fill someone else's shopping list, I had to develop an attitude and a system that would accommodate other people's input while leaving me in charge to the degree that I could get some satisfaction from realizing my own vision (which I felt was based on historical and artistic truths and a love of what the costume department could bring to the screen in terms of illustration).

I got my chance when I worked with a director named John Milius who believed in me enough to offer me a position as costume designer on a film he was to shoot in Spain. *The Wind and the Lion* is still one of my favorite movies to watch.

That was over twenty-five years ago. Since then I have worked on many films, television Movies of the Week (MOWs), pilots, and series as both costumer and costume designer. In practical terms, that means that I've had thousands of opportunities to make decisions about what people would wear on film and have been able to see the effects of those choices on the screen.

I've had the opportunity to supervise wardrobe departments in several foreign countries and several states on location. I've owned my own business and overseen the manufacture of hundreds of garments. I've also worked for several large costume houses as in-house shopper, buyer, designer, stock department head, and/or head of rentals and costumers' service.

I've also made mistakes at every level of job I've ever had, but, like the experience of most people, those mistakes taught me valuable lessons about both myself and my job.

Today the business is different from when I started; the studios don't have the large departments that they used to, nor do they make the volume of product themselves, so the training ground isn't there anymore for up-and-coming people to learn the ropes from an older generation of seasoned professionals. A lot of the people I see today struggle through shows because of this lack of opportunity for mentorship. That's why I've written this book.

I don't know if I can help anyone do a better job, or if I can really give anyone the benefit of my experience, but I'm happy to try... after all, we're all in the same department.

CHAPTER ONE

WORKING TOGETHER: COSTUME DESIGNER AND COSTUME SUPERVISOR OVERVIEW

Costume design is a collaborative effort, and I found that working with a variety of talented designers has been one of the best aspects of the business.

On the first Planet of the Apes *(1967), the designer, Morton Hack, wanted to create something really different for the "human tribe." They were supposed to be remnants of a civilization that had lost everything. He didn't want to use leather or fur because it would give them too much of a "cave man" look and suggest a level of aggression and hunting skill that the docile people in the script didn't have. By the same token, they didn't have the technology to weave cloth either, and putting them in grass-made anything would look too much like island natives... what to do? Weeks went by. The ape clothing was coming along okay, he had designed their civilization using a color scheme separation for the various groups; but this "human" thing wouldn't go away. We started to run out of preparation time and he knew he had to come up with something. One day, he came into the department all smiles. He said that he had gone to Santa Monica Beach over the weekend and had seen the city tree-trimming the palm trees on the palisades. He looked at that palm bark and knew he had his answer. The city of Santa Monica sold us a truckload of palm bark. It's a brown, fibrous substance that strips off the tree in small sheets. It's flexible, organic, and unlike anything else. We covered dress forms with plastic trash bags, then draped rough garment shapes with natural colored, course woven, silk drapery material. When the shape was finished, we painted on barge cement and stuck on the palm bark, finishing with a modeled paint job using leather spray. The finished garments looked great, and unlike any material you could think of or recognize.*

1

First things first.

Like any social adventure, running a department on production is a study in relationships. The first relationship, and in my book, the most important, is the relationship between designer and supervisor.

I cannot stress too much the importance of this partnership because from this union of skill and responsibility all things, department-wise, will flow. If this relationship starts badly or is a mistake, every other decision during the course of the production will be built on this mistake.

Like any relationship, the one of designer and supervisor has a human dimension of strengths and weaknesses that makes a universal absolute description or definition impossible, but the general rule is: the designer decides what the "look" is, and the supervisor makes it happen, i.e., the designer does the art and the supervisor does the business.

Let me give you some history about the wardrobe department. During the studio system days, every studio lot had its own wardrobe department presided over by a studio department head, who knew the stock available and the capability and cost of manufacture at lot labor prices. They also maintained lot department wardrobe crews who worked show to show, and knew who the best people were according to their experience and "touch."

When the studio decided to make a movie they gave the script to the department head who read it, broke it down, and then perhaps had a meeting with the senior wardrobe folks to get their feeling for the production requirements, costume availability, and any hidden obstacles or expensive scenes.

The movie was graded as an "A" film or a "B" film. If it were an "A" picture then everyone knew it would enjoy a big-name cast and have an expensive director and producer attached, and that would mean more money for the below-the-line segment of production. If that were the case, then the department would hire a costume designer to develop specific costumes. Usually that would mean dresses for the leading lady, but it could mean changes for the leading man, and even complete head-to-toe design concepts for everyone who appeared before camera — depending on the scope, period of the show, available costumes for rent, etc.

In large-scale period dramas there might be more than one designer — one overall, one for jewelry, one for certain characters, etc. Many times the designer was from Broadway and was heavily experienced in things theatrical; other times the designer was from the world of courtier. Often they were selected because of their area of expertise and how it could contribute to the type of show or star involved, and if the job of the costume designer were finished before the picture, then the designer left early. It was the costume department head who ran the wardrobe side of the production through the wardrobe supervisor. If it were a "B" film (or most television) then the wardrobe supervisor did it all without a designer, and this bred some very talented and artistic wardrobe people who did very accomplished shows with costume skill and the director as the only source of inspiration.

All this changed in the late sixties and seventies. This was the time of the rise of the independent production company. The studio lot was seen as too expensive, and the door was open for small film companies to put shows together on a wide assortment of money deals and shoot mainly on location. Many of these shows avoided costume designers as too expensive and dedicated to manufacture, and hired experienced costume supervisors recruited from studio lots to head their costume departments. This was the heyday of the creative independent supervisor, who had to develop new skills to facilitate the financial conditions on independent films.

In the days when films were on the lot, we as supervisors were never concerned with budgets, as they were all handled at the production level between department head and producer. With the rise of the indies, supervisors who found themselves in charge of wardrobe departments on production, had to keep the budget in sync with the production auditor under the direction of the unit production manager. The UPM was responsible to the producer to make the film for a certain budget, and all the department heads were responsible to the UPM for their department expenditures. Supervisors gained a new fiscal responsibility and with it the development of a new more business-like consciousness for what things cost and the most effective and cost-efficient way to do their jobs.

With the eighties and nineties two new types of production arose: music videos and large-budget commercials. With this new, mostly youthful, and extra Hollywood market came the stylist. Production companies hired anyone who could do the job to provide the "look." Some, without the prior constraints of a union job division mentality, and a desire to succeed in a creative field, took off and did makeup-wardrobe or some other hyphenated job, but many applied themselves to their costume vocation and have since broken into motion pictures and television as designers.

The market today has never been better for the trade of costume designer. Virtually every film, major and minor, lists a credit for costume designer, as do most TV shows... but where does a person learn the practical production side? The major lots and their departments are gone (in the old sense) and most production people are too young to remember how things were once organized. It's one thing to have talent, inspiration, imagination, and dedication, but it's another thing to be able to organize them into a system that is capable of sustaining you on a show with the most amount of efficiency and the least amount of hardship.

Nowadays the designer is usually hired first and given the title and responsibility of department head, but what does that mean? The designer must be concerned first and foremost with the look of the costumes; anything that takes away from, or interrupts that focus, is not part of costume design but part of department supervision. The costume designer, if hired first, is the de facto department head and nobody will argue with that, but that doesn't mean that the designer has to, or should want to, micromanage the day-to-day activities of the department. That's the job of the supervisor. The province of the costume designer is the workroom, and the province of the costume supervisor is the department labor, facility, and set operations; but they must collaborate on the department budget and its administration.

The department must be set up to handle the workload. On any show, production problems will come at you daily, so the best thing you can do about it is to always be prepared. That means having a system that encourages team work, team spirit, and quick reaction time; it requires a commitment to constant awareness; and the development of evenhanded and nontempermental managerial skills.

The designer must provide the decisions that make the work possible. The designer should lead from the front, defending the department in the knowledge that everyone hired is hired only to support the aesthetic decisions of the designer. After all, if no help were hired, the designer would have to work alone, so the designer, to be most effective, must always appreciate, encourage, and inspire the department labor to accomplish a vision.

With regard to the workroom, the designer must do research and drawings, and give instructions — obtaining materials, supplies, whatever it takes, because the cutter-fitters and stitchers are there only to consummate the designer's vision in cloth. So if it's not right, it's not their fault. It's the fault of the designer for not giving complete instructions or not checking the progress of work for potential mistakes.

The supervisor, who is second in command, runs the department — supervises the department's day-to-day operations, hires and fires, assembles the costumes, secures department space, facilitates the designer's decisions, and oversees the dressing of extras, department logistics, paperwork, and budget.

The designer and the supervisor work together like the metaphysical principle of the ethereal and the material, or the spirit and the letter, or like that well-known "right brain/left brain" relationship. One half of the brain thinks in artistic, conceptual terms, while the other half thinks in terms of organization and mathematics, but both sides are necessary and both sides must communicate with each other for anything to be accomplished. Remember, the most inspired artistic concept is impotent without a physical means of expression, and by the same token, all the tightly wound systems of organization ever invented are meaningless without aesthetic inspiration.

So, while the designer is the department head and in charge, the responsibilities must be shared with a strong costume supervisor. The two must collaborate so that the department will be capable of dealing with all the disquietudes of production that are sure to follow.

Once this fundamental relationship is established, then everyone will know what to do. After all, most people want to be successful at their jobs, want to be recognized as good workers, and pleasing to their boss. The first step in being good at your job is understanding your assignment clearly so you know what to be good at. The other thing is that a clear understanding of job definition means that you can divide the worry, you can BOTH plan everything together. One person has the responsibility to follow through on one area while the other person follows through on another; when problems come to the department, you'll know where to throw them.

By the way, there is a new kind of supervisor appearing, the executive, accountant type. These computer-literate folks spend less and less time with the costumes and more and more time with the computer. They are constantly in the process of updating the paperwork side of the department with spread sheets and budget predictions. I believe that this is in reaction to the huge budgets of Hollywood productions, and the accountants' and producers' constant need to know where they are financially. The supervisor position may evolve away from the department in the physical sense, or maybe the necessity for a wardrobe accountant position, as an integral job within the department, may develop as a response to the evolving fiscal responsibilities in productions. But for now, computer literacy is becoming a job requirement for supervisors.

CHAPTER TWO

GETTING STARTED:
BREAKING DOWN THE SCRIPT

I was on a Western in Arizona. One night I was helping check in extras. The men were all coming in without hats. Now I knew I gave them hats that morning, and the L/D price on a Western hat was about $150.00 each, so I started asking them where their hats were. The answer, "The second AD told us to take them off for the last shot, so we left them on the set." I went back to the set and found most, but not all of them. I went to the second AD and told him what I thought; that he had no authority or reason to misuse my department's equipment; that if he wanted to create some "wardrobe gag," he should have the decency to tell someone from our department so we could retrieve our gear; and that this lapse in judgment cost the company over a thousand dollars. He agreed, he'd told the extras to remove their hats and never thought a thing about it; he was sorry. But I still had to pay for the missing hats.

Breaking down a screenplay involves both the designer and supervisor. Everybody's job starts here.

You read the script with two objectives in mind:

- **FIRST** *To assess the requirements for the department.* Both designer and supervisor are interested in the same things: How big is the project? What's the period? What's the level of drama? The difference is that the designer sees and thinks in terms of color, detail, maybe even specific costumes, while the supervisor is more interested in crowd size, size of cast, length of schedule, and difficulty of locations.

- **SECOND**   *To arrive at a department budget.* That is, to try and predict a final cost that can be discussed with the producers and accountants.

Another way to think of your breakdown package is this: let's say that you were going into a business of your own. It's a start-up operation. You want to borrow money from the bank to fund your idea. You'll be the CEO. Your idea is to design, manufacture, and retail a line of clothing. You will need: a diverse staff to perform many and varied functions, as well as office space and supplies, warehouse space and fixtures, manufacture space and equipment, transportation, and shipping and receiving. You anticipate hundreds of pieces of inventory to rotate through your facility daily, requiring a maintenance operation. Your expenditures will be ongoing, requiring some sort of in-house accounting system. Your operation would exist over time, in various phases, each having its own related costs, and required expertise.

No matter how great a creative genius you are, before any bank will lend you any money to pursue your idea, they would demand that you submit, for their approval, a business plan, which would have to show:

  1. That YOU understood what you were getting yourself and them into, regarding time and money.

  2. That YOU were able to manage the work that you were suggesting.

Well, that's exactly what you're doing when you break down a script.

Heading up a large department for a film company has all the same challenges and responsibilities as going into a small business, with employees, inventory, payroll, physical work space... through time. So, to a large degree, the requirements that banks and businesses demand — financial responsibility combined with job insight — are demanded also by the producers and accountants, who act as the "bank" on every film.

This is more true now than it used to be when we department personnel were cloistered from the "business" of the films we worked on; but the good news is that there are various business plan concepts that are adaptable to your department head job... and it's not as hard as I'm making it sound.

8

Okay, you're sitting at home, you had a great meeting with the producer and you've been hired. You now have a fresh screenplay in your hands and are excited because it validates you as a real costume professional, it represents another stepping stone in your career, and you get to pay your rent for another three months. Well, what now?

Read it.

That's right, no pressure, just read it.

Your first reading of the script should be as innocent as the audience that will see it later. Scribble some notes: general impressions, things that stood out one way or another, what the story was about, what stood out about the main characters, and any serious questions.

By the end of the script you should have a good gut feeling about what kind of film it is, how serious it is, the level of drama, what periods and locations it covers, and how big a production it is.

That overview will form the mental background for your subsequent discussions about the story with anyone. In fact, a little later, you will want to cross-check your impressions with the producer and director to be sure that they see it the same way you do. That will constitute a very important CONCEPT meeting wherein questions about the visual style and the reasoning behind it, can and will be answered, and you will be set on the right track with full knowledge of what's expected of you and your department.

Start to build a foundation on paper that will serve as reference material for everyone and everything that follows until the end of production, which will include: breakdowns, research, and budget. This is your Costume Department Business Plan.

Just a word about personal style. I still work with a pencil and paper and that's how I'll explain things... but, if you're computer literate, all my information will transfer to a computer spreadsheet format. In spite of computers, I like to see everything spread out on a table in front of me as I work on it. I tend to build it visually and physically at the same time.

On a computer I can only see the page I'm working on until I print them out... too long for me to wait.

I do two master breakdowns; the first is on a yellow tablet, a CHRONOLOGICAL BREAKDOWN, i.e., I list the scenes in order by sequence. A sequence is a series of scenes that take place together; when the scenes change location or time, it's a new sequence. In each sequence I list the cast members that appear as well as the types of backgrounds and a guess at the number of extras. I also list, briefly, the action and weather, if a factor. This breakdown will serve as a template for subsequent costume lists from which my budget will be derived.

While doing this breakdown I become very familiar with the story, sequence of events, cast, plot points, mood, and action, as well as locations and what main dramatic point the writer is trying to convey. In other words, *What kind of film is it? How serious is it? How big is it?* All with an eye to how it should look.

The next breakdown I make is called a CROSSPLOT. It's made on graph paper and is very easy to do. A few lines across the top create categories that correspond to scene headings in the script: LOCATION, DAY/NIGHT, INTERIOR/EXTERIOR, SCENE NUMBER. Down the vertical left-hand margin I number one through twenty (sometimes on larger shows I have to tape two pieces together and number down to fifty or more). Each number will correspond to an actor's "cast number" which the first assistant director will have on the strip board and which will appear on every daily call sheet under "cast requirements."

Now I read the script again, filling in the information boxes across the top of the page, and the cast down the vertical column. When I find that an actor works in a particular scene, I put a slash in the box under that scene number. When there is a change of time, I separate that scene number from the next one with a vertical red pencil line. Soon the whole show is separated into chronological units. You can see at a glance, in which scenes a character works, how many changes (day changes) they have, and who else is in the scene. You can see the flow of the show as well as the continuity from interiors to exteriors. You can see where your extra crowds are and when the stunts work. You can photocopy it and post it in the department as a guide and reminder for what your department is working to achieve. You can post it in the truck on location and check the call sheet against it for continuity. And you can use it to pull your next set of breakdown sheets.

The next set of breakdown sheets are called the CAST BREAKDOWN sheets. They are for the people that need to be specifically costumed. You'll need separate sheets for:

- **MAIN CAST** These are the main characters in the story.

- **SECONDARY CAST** These people have large pivotal parts but appear less often, in cameo or featured running parts.

- **FEATURED BITS** They may have only one line, but it's written and the camera will be on them, so they form a part of the visual tapestry.

- **SILENT BITS** They may never have a line but are a featured part of a principal group (e.g., the drunk that falls down in the bar, a posse member, or the silent group around the chief). They take direction from the director instead of the assistant director.

- **THE STUNT PLAYERS** Sometimes these people form a large part of the cast, as in, "the bad guy's gang." Most often they blend into the background and appear as extras who get killed, or sometimes they appear only as doubles for cast members.

The reason for this breakdown is to isolate the individual changes for the players so that they may be assessed, budgeted, accumulated, and kept track of through their work until the end of production.

This set of breakdown sheets will become "the set book" which will record the life of each major costume on the show and provide a guide for matching the continuity of an actor's change through a jumbled production schedule. They are usually notebook-size forms divided into three or four horizontal boxes. Each box lists, in chronological order, the change number according to the scene number of an actor's clothing (For instance, "JOE BLOW, CHANGE #1, SCENE #s 1–5, INT.

SALOON, DAY" goes into the first box, and a description of the change follows such as "Change #1-Black #1 hat w/silver band, black shirt and pants, tooled boots").

This is done for every character and every change. If the change is repeated EXACTLY its scene number can go in the same box, but if the change is altered slightly for another segment it's given the same number with a letter reference, 1A, 1B, etc. so that information such as "doubled for stunt," "gets wet" or "progressive aging" goes in the appropriate box. Soon we can get a good sense of the amount of NECESSARY costumes the show needs to shoot the main characters and their story. From these character change sheets, one can determine how many costumes the players will need, when to have multiples (for stunts, damage, excessive use) and whether the costumes will have to be made, purchased, or rented.

During production, the day an actor first works in a scene, the outfit is recorded on Polaroid film (as it plays in the scene); the picture taped in the book with a brief description of how the clothes were worn (e.g., "collar open"). A permanent record is developed, scene by scene, change by change, actor by actor, so that in the event of retakes or having to match clothing from interior to exterior, shots at different times, or in case there are changes in wardrobe personnel, one will always know who wears what and how it was worn.

By the way, some very up-to-date set people nowadays are photographing costume shots on the set with a digital camera, printing the photo out from the computer, and then mounting the color 8½" x 11" in clear plastic three-ring document holders for the set book.

Now's the time to look for "multiples." Multiples are figured in the event that one set of clothes for a given change is deemed insufficient. It's always a good idea to have at least doubles in shirts, ties, hats, and dresses for your cast just in case of sweat, makeup slip, lunch spill, other unforeseen disasters, or if your location is in a place where overnight cleaning is impossible. In the event that your overall budget is small, this isn't always possible, but if the change "works a lot," that is, if a particular change of clothing is seen a lot on screen, at least try to double the part that is seen closest on camera, usually the clothes surrounding the face.

Another situation that demands doubles is inclement WEATHER. Let's say that Bill the sailor, your cast member, works on the deck of a ship during a rainstorm in a long action sequence. Two or three complete changes for Bill and two or three for his stunt double may do it; in addition the stunt double may be a different size from the actor, he may have to wear special shoes for the wet deck and oversized clothes to hide a wetsuit underneath.

As you can see, the above scene will call for a lot of preparation, communication, work, and money. Find out the cost of wetsuits, have a chat with the stunt coordinator about the scope of the stunt and sizes of the stunt man, then get ready to query the director about how the scene will be shot — because all the information you acquire will be needed when you have a "money talk" with the line producer.

Another example of demanding doubles might be the LOCATION. If your shoot will be in and around a lot of water, streams, swamps, rainy areas, you can bet that your cast will get wet at some point, needing extra footwear, socks, and even pants and skirts.

STUNTS are always a factor. Extra clothing for the stunt doubles should always be checked on with the stunt coordinator. Also, sometimes the stunt requires that the stunt person wear protective clothing, harnesses, and have fireproofing done. These things are not strictly thought of as part of the "costume look" of a show, and are sometimes overlooked until late in the preparation period, or on location when the last thing you'll need is more things to invent or acquire. So plan accordingly.

Another reason for multiples of changes is PROGRESSIVE AGING. Let's say that your characters are lost in the jungle for a period of time and we see them degenerate on screen. In the beginning they look like they stepped right out of the city, next they look rumpled and a little soiled, next they get dirty and start to get torn, last they are in filthy rags. How many sets of doubles? Well, if there are four main stages to the aging, four sets might do it; if stunts are involved then perhaps eight or more duplicates will be required. On *Rambo III*, I had over thirty duplicates for Mr. Stallone even though it was the same black "U" shirt and cargo pants: there was Stallone himself, plus three stunt doubles and the change worked every day for months, constantly being washed,

13

over-dyed, damaged, and repaired in order for it to always look the same on camera at the right time.

SPECIAL EFFECTS is a department that is required to be hard on clothes. Usually "squibs" (bullet hits), "fire gags," and "water gags" are their province also. They always want to have two or three garments available to them to destroy, per gag, apart from the changes you need for costuming the show. On big effects productions, this can run into the hundreds of garments. Here, after you realize the scale of destruction you can determine whether it will be more cost-efficient to manufacture, purchase, or rent the costumes you need to destroy.

Another consideration is the decoration and property department. Technically, when an actor removes his hat or coat in a scene it becomes an "action prop" and most prop people will inquire if you plan to have the described item there that day or not. Sometimes they will want to "hold" the item if it works the next day. But I always keep principle wardrobe locked in my truck, on stage, or in the department.

It's a good idea to check with the decorator as to whether there are plans to use any wardrobe for set dressing, i.e., in closets or drawers, on clothes lines, at the site of a wreck, or whatever. If so, I explain to the decorator that I'm only bringing enough wardrobe to do the changes of the actors, so if they need wardrobe I will rent what they want and pass it on to them. I like decorators, and have decorated sets myself, but they will always use the clothes you give them with casual abandon, strewing them about rooms or hanging them on exterior clothes lines (in the rain, no matter)... and when they're done with them they will, sometimes, return them dirty, or stuffed into boxes or paper bags. So please, spare yourself the agony, get them what they need so as not to interfere with the costumes that are available to YOU to do the job YOU have to do.

Once you have arrived at the wardrobe requirements for the cast, you can use this information to project an individual cast cost that can be plugged into your budget. You can also begin to get an idea of the size of the crew required and the type of expertise you will need to hire.

The next (and last) set of breakdowns has to do with BACKGROUND. Going back to the Chronological Breakdown we can now pull a list of background requirements together. This set of breakdowns, when finished, will give you a basis for discussion of department requirements and their cost with anyone, and will enable you not only to reach an overall cost figure but to assemble costumes (should you be dealing with a costume house). This set of breakdowns becomes a large part of my department budget.

When you read the script, you have to read between the lines. In any dramatic presentation, the story concerns the cast playing out the drama, as they move through a series of locations, time, and background crowds. The question is, how are these crowds composed (size and type) and how much will it cost to do them? The scene says "TRAIN STATION — DAY." The key players meet on the platform, talk and walk away. When you read the scene, what do you see? If it's a "normal day" there might be a hundred or more people there. Every script is different, but by now you should have a feel for the scale of your production (at this stage production people may not be available or the decisions about extra counts may not have been made). Take your best guess, call it a hundred if you feel that's about right (you'll be able to change it later when there is more information from the production office). Now, list the hundred in the background by type. What kind of people would be in a train station — what's going on in your story? Let's say it's The Old West, twenty couples, better dress – day wear, that's forty people, plus ten "train types," e.g., conductors and red-caps, and maybe ten soldiers on leave, plus ten cowboys, five blanket Indians, that's seventy-five, now add ten Mexican types, five nuns, five salesmen in plaid suits, and five trappers in leathers. Okay, that's a hundred people with a little variety and an Old West flavor. Now, do that for every set, keeping in mind what types would best sell that period, location, mood, to the audience. When you're satisfied that you've accounted for most or all the major types of costumes that you'll need on your show, then start a page for each group.

PAGE ONE, MEN, COWBOYS, 100 OUTFITS.
100 Hats, Western character
100 Hat bands, asst., leather, horse hair
100 Bandannas, various print and plain, cotton, silk
 50 Long John tops, over-dyed
100 Shirts, long sleeve, assorted
100 Vests, wool, assorted

50 Coats, wool, 4-button, asst.
50 Coats, outer, mackinaw, wool, assorted
100 pr. Suspenders
50 Belts, wide
100 pr. Pants, wool, cotton asst. top pocket
25 pr. Chaps, leather
50 pr. Cuffs, leather
100 pr. Boots, Western
25 Slickers, oilcloth, yellow
50 pr. Spurs

PAGE TWO, WOMEN, SALOON GIRLS, 15 OUTFITS.
15 Hair trimmings, feathers, sequins
15 "Saloon Girl" dresses, asst.
15 Shawls, silk
15 pr. Hose, black-ribbed or net
15 Corsets, white, boned
15 Camisoles, white ctn. with ribbon trim
10 pr. Gloves, black evening
15 pr. Leg Garters, elastic
15 pr. Shoes, period, high-lace
15 sets "foundation" wear (as per dresses)

As you do this you will find that you may not need shoes for every person in every crowd, only to cover your largest amount. You might want more hats than outfits so the clothes become more versatile; black suits and dresses might work both for a funeral crowd and for a train station scene.

You might to want to have a 10% allowance of clothes over what you think you need, for "fitting stock."

You will begin to see the clothes as units, building blocks that can be combined and recombined to get the desired effect in each set throughout the production. Use your imagination.

Once you have developed these sheets, you can price each group according to their point of origin (rentals, purchases, or manufacture).

You now have an inventory list that you can discuss with the line producer for direct cost as well as the amount of time and wardrobe labor necessary for preparation. You can talk to the director about ambiance, confer with the first assistant director about atmosphere amounts, and look to your own department for the amounts and types of stock to be developed, with a built-in check-list to double-check in case something has been overlooked.

At this point, you also have a basis for a discussion with any costume house in the world as far as availability of stock, pricing, and constructing a package deal. You can also develop a shopping list for outside vendors and costume makers.

Other items that will affect your budget thinking will be: SECOND UNIT and SCHEDULE.

"Second Units" are common on action films and composed mostly of stunt people and extras. This unit can greatly expand your department requirements for rentals and labor, especially if shot concurrently with First Unit, Principal Photography.

Schedule information will help you schedule your department's labor and acquisition of costumes. You might find that you have more time for manufacture if the clothes work later in the shooting schedule; but never plan too heavily around the shooting schedule. If they change their minds you're in trouble.

CREW REQUIREMENTS   Will you be required to have safety gear or protective clothing for the crew? Hats for the sun, waders for water work? Some companies understand that weather or other conditions will necessitate a certain amount of company-provided crew wear and will have you put it in the budget; other companies will not want to spend the money on these items. If they do, I always ask Production to send a memo to each department head requesting what items they want and the sizes, then give these items over to the departments on a *one-time* basis. If they don't want to spend the money, then I ask production to publish a letter to the crew, informing them that the company will not be responsible for crew-needed items and that they have to provide their own. This heads off potential bad feelings later on.

RESEARCH AND DEVELOPMENT   "R and D," as it's called, is money reserved to pay for research, to obtain sample fabrics, to make or buy sample garments, to get outside pattern-making and grading, and to buy dye tests and materials, mould making, and the like. These are all things that contribute to your costume stock but aren't part of it.

A cautionary note: Take nothing for granted with regard to the availability or cost of costumes. Do research with phone calls, detailed descriptions, Polaroids and first-hand visits to costume rental houses BEFORE you commit to Production that you can deliver a show for a price. Never estimate what you think a costume house will charge you. Call and find out; there's always a chance that what you need won't exist for rent. Large shows regularly manufacture, and/or purchase, great amounts of costumes at various costume houses. Almost every costume house has the means and contacts for providing for any type of fabrication or purchase. They are always ready for a serious discussion about providing for your needs. More on this in Chapter 5.

DRESS EXTRAS AND REENACTORS   Sometimes, producers engage the services of dress extras or reenactors (living history folks). These are people that the producer feels can wear their OWN, usually home-made costumes in order to save money. While SOMETIMES, their uniforms are worth using (they're almost always too clean and bright, and because they are personal, you can't age them) their civilian clothes are sometimes a little disappointing. Lacking in a unified color scheme and exhibiting every level of manufacture, you will loose control over the composition of background crowds unless you are able to bring as much background clothing as you can, at least key and character pieces.

I have worked many shows with reenactors and some of them have worn really great outfits; but not all of them. So when I have this possibility suggested to me I always ask if the producers, who are spending millions of dollars on this screen project, really want the look of the picture left up to what an extra wears on any given day.

The next piece of information to add to your budget package is research. In reality, you start researching the period as soon as you know what the show is about, and it's the research that helps you develop the concept for both foreground and background. Years ago at Fox, the department head told me "I don't care what it is, if it's in the script I want to see a picture of it!" I found that to be good advice.

Nothing gives you a feeling for what you're doing like seeing it. Today there are many sources for conducting research. The traditional ones are libraries, studio or costume house research departments, art books, and older films; and now there is the Internet, where you even have the ability to scan a film into a computer and pull any still shot from it.

But before you start pulling research, think about how to use it. There are various ways to do a research package, but like a resume, "only show them what you want them to see," applies here.

Some people do extensive research into a period and later demand that every item be authentic. Other people take a more broad-brush view and are satisfied to capture some sense of general tone on the background and a more specific characterization on the featured players. Some prefer to use reality as a jumping-off point for a presentation more cartoonish or surrealistic (after all, the old adage says: "reality is the enemy of art"), but to be really helpful, research has to be very specific. I've seen people show photos of the wrong Indians or soldiers at the wrong time or battle because they looked "close." Sometimes this can lead to situations that are embarrassing, if confronted by someone on the production with the "right" research. Try to find images that show *exactly* what you're doing. You can always develop a costume concept that is at variance with reality, but you should still know what the reality is.

I like to do three types of research:

- **FIRST** Historical, that is, costume reference books that show line drawings of the clothes.

- **SECOND** Art book color photocopies, which show how artists of the period saw themselves and their surroundings, or how great illustrators depicted the period, and, of course, real photos when available.

- **THIRD** Textual, that is, printed regulations or historical first-hand descriptions related to what we're going to shoot.

Whatever the combination, research is vital in presenting the reasons for, and the substantiating historical documentation behind, your costume choices to Production people, some of whom will certainly have done research of their own.

I also have to admit, since I've worked as a costume house employee, nothing amazes me more than a costumer who comes to search out clothes for a show and isn't prepared with research. After all, it's YOUR show, YOU'RE the one getting paid to do it. I've always thought it a little unprofessional to take a job and then rely on a costume house employee to do your show for you. On the other side, most costume houses employ certain people for their specific knowledge, as in a "military expert" or a "period expert," and they are happy to help you arrive at the best, most authentic or realistic costumes available to you. The bottom line is, do your homework, and ask questions; but don't dump your job on someone else.

While doing your research, don't stop at the photographs. Years ago I learned that there were people, not of our department, who weren't shy about going to the director and questioning Wardrobe. I decided then that if I were going to take clothes to the set I was going to be able to answer any questions anybody might have about them, after all, the cameraperson can answer questions about the camera, film, and light; the key grip is conversant about construction and diffusion; well, if you're a costume person then clothes are YOUR TOOLS, so it's only professional and right that you know how to explain and use them.

Doing in-depth costume research is: necessary, time-consuming, illumi-nating, professional, entertaining, and fun. It broadens your base of knowledge and allows you to discuss your craft with intelligence while giving you new things to try.

By in-depth I mean reading history as it applies to culture and costumes in general. When was the Silk Trade with China; the importation of cheap cotton goods from India that almost caused a war between England and France; the Lace Wars between Germany and the Low Countries; what dye colors were popular and how were they made? What was the sense of style in this particular movie's world? In other words, what was the world like then? What did people have to work

20

with, and how did they use it? Being graced with understanding and knowledge will allow you to do better, more sure and confident work, and you'll be able to explain it to anyone, anytime.

The last artistic ingredients to the package are original costume sketches and swatches that "fill in the blanks" where the cast is concerned. Sketches are funny things that intimidate many, including those who have little or no faith in their own artistic ability. Usually they aren't as hard as they seem. We'll talk more about them and how to do them later.

Swatches are a good tool for a visual presentation because they bring their own beautiful reality of texture and color. Some people mount them according to each character, some to give an impression of what a crowd might look like. Sometimes they serve as samples for real manufacture with yardage counts and prices attached.

Accumulation of swatches is a great learning experience necessary to any costumer or designer interested in the direct tools of costume construction. During the process of swatch accumulation you will discover new sources and fabrics (which can be an unexpected source of inspiration) while learning about the availability of materials and the limitations of local sources.

When combined with your breakdowns and budgets, research, including an art package, will give you a complete reference tool that can help guide your department, because you'll be getting everyone on the same page (literally). You'll be able to answer questions and settle disputes regarding historical accuracy, and you'll have a sound basis for discussions about money, manufacture, or escalating costs necessitated by production changes.

Just to recap, you should now have:

1. **A CHRONOLOGICAL BREAKDOWN** describing the script, sequence by sequence, with your guess on background types and amounts.

2. **A COSTUME CROSSPLOT** on graph paper, showing you the whole movie at a glance, giving you all the scene numbers and showing which actor works where.

3. **ACTOR CHANGE SHEETS** a series of pages with every costume change described for every actor, noting multiples and the related budget information.

4. **BACKGROUND BREAKDOWN SHEETS** another series of pages, one for each type of background costume needed, with all the items described and priced for your budget with page totals.

5. **RESEARCH PACKAGE** with photos, photocopies, and designer sketches, showing the period, types of costumes historically worn and/or specifically designed, and swatches showing colors and fabrics that can be used and to what effect.

Before we get to the next part of the budget, the labor part, let's look at feature budgets in general.

In the old days, when a feature was started at the studio, they had a position called the estimator. Many of these senior accountants had worked for years in studio accounting and had reviewed budget after budget, Westerns, war movies, cops and robbers, comedies. They had the luxury of watching how the money was spent by each lot department over a long period of time, and could, with great accuracy, estimate what a film should/would cost based upon their experience. Often they knew your problems before you did and could advise the producer to "plug" money into the budget against sometimes not-so-obvious situations that experience told them were likely to arise.

Armed with this experience and input from the studio department heads, the producer could develop a show budget that was largely based on the realities of production requirements, and the final budget was a product of the film's requirements. Sadly, this position is largely gone.

There is another way for producers to figure a show budget, and it's a way that's used very often, especially on lower-budgeted films. It's called the percentage budget, and it has no basis in the realities of the production requirements written in the script. It is an uninformed formula that producers hope to stay within. It can be your biggest obstacle to success and a constant source of argument, but if it's the reality, then you have to understand it.

Unit managers and producers are accountable for the money, to whatever source gave it to them. Most studio productions have deep pockets, that is, if it costs more money than was first thought, they will generally come up with the shortfall rather than risk their investment. Independents have no such luck, mostly working on negative pick-up deals or a specific amount of raised money based on projected sales, so there are no deep pockets to go back to for more money. In this situation the budget is a product of available production funds.

Unlike independent film budgets, the percentage budget is constructed the other way around. Instead of figuring out what things will cost and raising the money to fund them, the money raised is split among the various departments by a formula percentage, so a "this is what I'm willing to pay" mentality governs the show. Needless to say, this can be very frustrating when you start to develop a projection of what you think of as your real expected costs only to find yourself way over budget.

The only way to have a realistic budget discussion with producers and production managers is to have all your costs documented. If it's more than they want to spend or can spend, you will be able to arrive at compromises with them relating to the production requirements written in the script. For this reason, an insightful and clear budget is demanded.

A long time ago a producer told me that no one ever did anyone a favor by turning in a budget that was too light. As my old Chinese grandfather used to say, "Things that come too cheap in the beginning come too expensive in the end."

The next part, the LABOR BUDGET, is easy to construct.

Start with a piece of graph paper.

Number down the left-hand margin as many jobs as you think you will have: DESIGNER, ASSISTANT DESIGNER, SUPERVISOR, LEAD COSTUMER, KEY SET, TRUCK PERSON (including day labor), AGING PERSON, DYER, ASST. DYER (manufacture labor), CUTTER, STITCHER, MILLINER (location help), LAUNDRY PERSON, LOCATION ALTERATION TAILOR, etc.

You want to list any and all jobs that will be paid by your company's payroll and work directly for you. Do not include vendors, as they have already been accounted for in the CAST or BACKGROUND manufacture and purchase part of your budget.

Now, estimate the preparation weeks necessary, travel time to location (in weeks), location shooting weeks, wrap weeks, return shipping time, and final return period.

Count this time in weeks, at a square per week across the paper from left to right after the job positions. This budget page will look similar to your Crossplot.

The next thing is to figure who will work how long. The DESIGNER, for example, might work the entire show, so put a slash in every square for prep period, production period, and wrap period; the key set person may only work one or two weeks of an eight-week prep, for the entire shooting period, and then have no wrap time, so mark the squares accordingly.

This is where you really have to consider everything that may happen to your show, such as how much help you need to get the costumes together, how much set labor to work the shoot, how much of it local, and what kind of department capabilities are necessary on location. If preparing at a costume house, will your deal include any costume house labor?

Now you have a series of time period squares behind each job, each of them checked for the amount of weeks that each person is expected to work.

Somehow arrive at the pay level for your show. This may be union scale plus an overtime allowance, or a flat rate allowance. Whatever it is, make it realistic; remember, you're not doing anybody a favor by submitting unrealistically low numbers out of fear or hope. Put the weekly pay amount in each square behind the correct job heading, run the numbers and you should have an estimate for the labor cost of your show, person-by-person, job-by-job and phase-by-phase.

24

The last thing we need to consider for your budget are the items that comprise DEPARTMENT OVERHEAD. These are the expenses that typically accompany a costume department but are easily overlooked.

For example, when you shoot on the lot and you need something done for a costume you can take it back to the department. Alterations? No problem, there's a tailor shop. Hat doesn't fit? No problem, if there's not a hat shop, there is a floor steamer and a set of blocks. Need something dyed? Easy, write it up and send it to the cleaners.

Many people have never had the opportunity to see a full-service wardrobe department function, much less been blessed with the back-up that such a department offers. Starting on small projects or non-union shows forces most people to learn the ropes by crisis, but the good news is that the work of the wardrobe department never changes, and once you learn to provide for it in your thinking it's as easy as ABC. Well, almost.

It might be a good idea to conjecture a little about some of the problems usually faced by our department so that we can form some general insights to help guide our assessment.

Think down your outfits from head to toe; HATS, WEARING APPAREL, SHOES. That's all there is. Now, after you assemble these items, how will you work with them? (And that means service them.)

They will have to live in a department of some kind. There has to be storage space, some kind of physical department. This might mean the trunk of your car, a rental warehouse or a truck, or a combination thereof.

You have to think about the location and the location conditions, and decide how best to provide for the physical space in which you need to work. On a large feature it's not uncommon to have a central warehouse, or rooms at the local motel, feeding one truck or more. Or you can work the show out of a large (40-foot) trailer with a hard-wall department back in town for storage and workroom, and a large tent on location to dress extras.

Once stored, the daily process will (almost always) be:

- The working clothes will travel to the set on a daily basis.
- Actors and extras will be fitted and dressed.
- Set operation through the shooting period.
- Daily maintenance/alterations.
- Clothes returned.
- Cleaning/pressing, most often overnight.
- Stock work in readying for the next day.

In addition, you may be building costumes on location and have to provide for some scale of workroom setup.

You will need some kind of provision for a bill-paying, record-storing office.

Before you can come up with a department overhead budget, you have to assess the workload on your show and develop a list of purchases for the expendable supplies and equipment that will be necessary due to the work you have planned or foresee, taking into account each phase of department work.

PREPARATION

Office:
    Space at a costume house, rental warehouse, truck interior, or home. General office supplies; computer, file box, paper supplies, copy ability, telephone/fax, cell phone/pager, office furniture, refrigerator, coffeemaker, lighting.

Department:
    Physical space for accumulating costumes. Clothing pipe racks; rentals, home-built, or purchased? How much rack space do you need in your department, on your truck, in the extra tent? Measure the clothes at a costume department or your closet; you can get about 100 shirts or dresses on one crammed six-foot rack, and fewer overcoats. While that might work for truck shipment, you can't

work that way. You might get only ten to fifteen complete outfits to a six-foot rack, or roughly, two, three, or four outfits, complete and hung together to the running foot (depending on how voluminous the costumes). So, that's about 100 feet of rack for every 400 outfits, maybe twice that for an extra dressing area where people have to sit and change side by side.

If every extra is allowed a foot as their own "closet" to hang their clothes, then the number of rack feet equals the number of extras (six-inch allowance, half as much).

You'll need rolling racks (purchase or rental?) to shuttle the costumes about. You might decide that the whole department will be better, portable, on rolling racks. Figuring the rack space needed to house your department, plus the rack space needed to dress extras, consider that this fact might result in a lot of rolling racks, with their own storage problems.

All this differs with the number of location moves your department has, the number of extras you're required to dress, and the size of the department you'll need to facilitate it all. Experience is the best teacher; you can find people who have done it before and have answers or ideas as to the best way to proceed.

Prices for rental racks can be obtained from any costume house, while the cost for building semi-permanent racks can be calculated by calling around for the raw material prices. Schedule forty galvanized pipe in $^3/_4$" has always worked the best for me, with 2 x 4s and $^3/_4$" CDX plywood used for the up-rights and bracing.

SUPPLIES
Hangers:
You'll need them every day. Plastic, wood, wire, clip, suit, dress? It's all personal preference, but for me, being raised the old way, I like wood (not for long-term storage where plastic is better, but for locations where strength counts). Start with a box... wire, I hate them, unless they're heavy-duty and coated. They're too weak, they rust, and leave marks in the clothes.

And all the usuals:

Shipping tags (for clothing sizes, alteration instructions, daily notes), safety pins, pens (Sharpies, markers, they go fast, get boxes), and string. Why string? We always were taught to hang the actor's footwear with the costume, with string, at the bottom of the hanging outfit; this takes about six to eight feet on the double. The reason? Well, you keep the outfit together, wherever it hangs, whenever it's moved. Why hang them low? So shoe polish won't get on the clothes and you can see them to make sure they're there, especially when on their way to the actor's dressing room. It also lets you keep your hands free when carrying more than one outfit. Use plastic shoe bags? Not unless dropped on a string, makes multiple outfits too bulky to carry.

Other supplies are dictated by how you like to work or set requirements. Some items might be: plastic garment bags, plastic shoe bags, electric floor or hand steamer, iron, electric or manual hat stretcher, and felt hat reducers.

I'm not going to try to list every type of supply available, since I have included a list of costume houses with supply stores in the back of the book (see Appendix, page 149).

On an average size Movie of the Week, expendable supplies can run two to three thousand dollars. On large features, several thousand.

WORKROOM

If you have to set up a shop to make your own garments, you have to consider the following: What are you asking them (the garment makers) to do? What level of skill and experience will it take? How many people will it take? Given the time and workload, what supplies will they need (sewing machines, hand tools, leather working equipment)? What will the shop have to look like in terms of furniture (cutting or work tables, lights)? What about raw material storage (shelving units, storage boxes)? What kind of space will it take to house that operation? Where will that space be located? Does it have enough natural light or will it need color-corrected fixtures? (You don't want to make any decisions regarding color of materials or dying under neon or other noncorrected light sources.) How's the air? Need fans, air conditioning, heaters? The answers might be simple or complex, cheap or very expensive depending on your show... but with each show, the questions and workroom provisions are the same.

I can tell you that on a Movie of the Week–size show where I've had two or three garment makers and/or alterations people, that shop costs between five hundred and a thousand a week in supplies for every week it's up and running, and that's not counting large material purchases.

If you estimate a large or unexpected workroom force, you might be asked to justify it.

The reasons are these:

- **FIRST** No matter the show, there will always be some things that are not rentable, not buyable, not findable, but they are things that will contribute mightily to the look of the show. Your only option is to make them yourself, under your own control and supervision.

- **SECOND** Alterations. Never in the history of filmmaking have all the cast members been fitted and approved in costume before shooting. You are sure to get some, even most of your cast, a day or two before they work. How will you get them fitted? Who will do the on-site manufacture and alterations?

- **THIRD** Equity. There will always be some loss and damage at the end of every show. Everything you make for yourself, like everything you buy for yourself, becomes a company asset. At the end of shooting you have developed stock that can be used to offset some or all of your L/D (loss and damage) and maybe even make a profit.

In the end, a well-planned workroom could pay for itself.

AGING/DYING/WASHING
Aging:

This is usually a thing you run into in war movies or Westerns. Let's say you're doing a military film. You have to make all the Japanese uniforms because they aren't available to rent, or you anticipate a lot of destruction so you want to avoid the huge and certain L/D bill from the rental facility at the end. So you make your five hundred Japanese uniforms... but they look too new, too fresh, these guys are supposed to look like they have been in the jungle for months, years. In other words, they have to be heavily distressed. Well, there's no easy way.

Start by thinking of the end result. These uniforms have to look used, dirty, ragged.

You might start by finding a local facility that does any of the following: sand wash, stone wash, enzyme, or acid wash. These are very good and fast methods for really breaking down clothes, but you must use caution. If the laundry doesn't use a bleach arrester on the final cycle, your clothes will look fine when you get them, but further washing or exposure to the sun will bleach them past where you want to go.

If you're working on a smaller scale try experimenting with fabric softener, bleach, and color remover. The first step is to soften the fabric and remove all the loose color (the color that will come out with a few washings).

The second step is to paint or over-dye the garments in an uneven fashion to resemble ground-in dirt. If you own the clothes and don't care, use paint if you like, but if the clothes are rented, use Fullers Earth (can be bought at any costume house) — either by itself (dry) or with mineral oil or Lexol or water. Rental houses take a dim view of returning their clothes with paint on them and you will surely pay.

When doing a medium-sized job on location, I mix a bath of Fullers Earth and water with a little brown dye, put it onto a large galvanized tub and give the garments a bath, then hang them on double hangers in the sun and squirt them from the top down with water and a little bleach, letting the sun do the rest.

The third step is the ragging. This can be done with anything from scissors and razor blades, to fish scalars and sandpaper, or you can beat holes into the fabric with a hammer on concrete or asphalt. I've known people who have thrown new cloths into a rented cement mixer with loose gravel or bricks.

How ever you choose to do it, it's labor-intensive and uncertain. You have to allow yourself extra garments for experimentation. I've seen shows where full-time aging staffs of ten-plus people labored for weeks to distress one group of costumes after another, using thousands of dollars of supplies.

WASHING

This is a constant job for Wardrobe. The only choice you have is how to do it. Department washer and dryer (more than one?), the local fluff and fold, the local commercial laundry, a laundromat, the washer at your location motel, or your bathtub. (Many a costumer has spent many an hour washing or dying clothes in the bathtub in their room on location.)

Whichever combination you choose will have a dollar amount attached to it. Three or four hundred a week is average to service the actors, cast, and background, plus five to ten thousand or more at the end when you return your show and everything has to be cleaned before being returned to stock.

DYING

This usually means "over-dying," but sometimes designers like to dye fabrics themselves for certain costumes. Only you know for sure on your show, but every dye operation needs hot water... washing machine, hot plate, and various pots and pans for fabric swatches. If you're going to do it, budget for it.

Note: You might also find helpful a color "chip" book from the local paint store, and a book on color theory from the local art store. Any book on color theory will help you understand color usage, but also, whatever it tells you about color mixing with paint will be true for dye also. (Ever thought of graying red by using green, or blue with orange, or yellow with purple?)

There are various kinds of dye available, Rit and Tintex are the two most widely used and can be found in any supermarket, but there are other dyes made for painting fabric. Inkodye is one of them. It will take a little research at a fabric or silk screen shop.

SHOOTING
Transportation:

While not strictly part of the costume budget, on small shows, you are all working out of one pot, so you have to consider how your costumes are going to be moved around and warehoused. If it's wheels on roads it's Transportation. I've also been on locations where the "tent camp" was provided by Transportation, so this could be where your extras change. Even if these requirements don't come out of your budget they come out of the Transportation budget, so go over your requirements with them. By the way, many costume houses own ready-to-roll wardrobe trailers for rent.

Under transportation you might also consider ground shipping. Going to order stuff from another state? Going to ship to another country? You might allow for UPS or FedEx for things sent around the States, but if you're going out of the country, you will have to come up with estimates on shipping boxes (costs) with an estimate of how many you will need, size, and what they will weigh when packed.

SET SUPPLIES

These supplies are sometimes supplied by costumers for a kit rental fee. If not, you'll have to supply tools for people to work with including scissors, pens, leather punches, a Leatherman tool and other small hand tools. In addition, you'll have a Polaroid camera, film, notebooks, toupee tape, two-faced tape, gaffer's tape, sewing kits, etc. I always used to give all my set people surplus military back-packs. I found that they're a good answer to carrying stuff around while keeping your hands free.

Next, you might think about things like robes, towels, socks, down jackets, extra thermal underwear, or extra straw hats for the sun. Part of your job is to have these supplies for the actors, but there will come the day when the crew, director included, will ask for a hat or coat.

WRAP
Cleaning:

Leather is the most expensive to clean, then wool, linen, and last, cotton. Women's things tend to be more expensive than men's. Extra money to hand-spot makeup or blood stains. Speaking of blood stains, you can help yourself in the beginning by adding liquid soap to whatever blood is being used and soaking the garment right away after the action.

PACKING
By box, or hanging in a truck? What's your expense?

Also, here you need to think about your return. There is a tendency in production to want to get everyone off payroll as soon as possible after shooting. To get all the rental items back to their point of origin and off rental as fast as they can. I understand this, but loss and damage will have its way if not addressed.

I was on a film in Mexico a few years ago. At the end of the show the producer wanted the wardrobe department to throw the clothes in boxes and get them back to the American rental houses within a few days after shooting to stop the rental.

It had been a long shoot and the clothes had taken a beating. Hanging on the racks they were dirty with many obvious repairs needed.

I pointed out that labor in Mexico costs less than labor in the United States, and suggested that we take two or three weeks in Mexico, with one American supervisor and a small Mexican crew, and wash, repair and line up the return — that is, assemble all the clothes in groups according to their billing sheet numbers. Done at this stage, we would see what was missing and would have the time to make or buy items that (hopefully) would be an acceptable exchange when the clothes reached the costume house. At the very least, we would learn what was missing and be able to prepare the producer for the bad news to come, but just washing and repairing the rental stock and doing an organized return would give the costume house little to charge for L/D. The producer disagreed; getting everyone off payroll was the priority.

The clothes were sent back. The costume house flipped out. They called the production company and refused to accept the return in its condition. Production had to rehire part of its American costume crew to unpack the boxes, sort the clothes according to billing sheets, have the clothes laundered and then address the cost of repairs, over sixty thousand dollars' worth. All in all that sloppy return cost the company close to ninety thousand dollars. Could all of that have been avoided by extending the wrap in Mexico? No, I'm sure not. Could some of it have been avoided? I'm sure so, by two-thirds anyway.

Speaking of L/D, I always plug in ten percent of my rental budget for eventual loss and damage. This includes items that have been destroyed during the course of filming and items that have been lost to theft or carelessness.

The finishing page is the COVER PAGE.

When you have finished your paperwork, put it all in order.

- **FIRST** Your cast sheets with their breakdowns and costs.

- **SECOND** Your background breakdown sheets with budget estimates.

- **THIRD** Your labor budget.

- **FOURTH** Your department overhead estimate.

- **FIFTH** Your research material. (An abbreviated research package is good to include as a budget addendum.)

Now, number the pages. List them, with their page totals, in numerical order. Last, total up the column, dividing and subtotaling by groups. It should look something like this:

Page 1.	cast, JOHN	$ 1,000.00
Page 2–3.	cast, MARTHA	$ 10,000.00
	(subtotal, cast)	**$ 11,000.00**
Page 4.	TOWNSPEOPLE, MEN	$ 40,000.00

Page 5.	TOWNSPEOPLE, WOMEN	$ 70,000.00
Page 6.	POLICE	$ 5,000.00
	(subtotal, B.G.)	**$115,000.00**
Page 7.	LABOR BUDGET	$ 50,000.00
Page 8.	DEPARTMENT OVERHEAD	$ 12,000.00
	total rentals =	**$126,000.00**
		Pages 1 through 6.
	show total =	**$188,000.00**

You can see that this gives you a well-designed budget tool for all the money meetings that will follow. You can, at a glance, look up and explain each increment of your budget, pull out specific details and adjust individual numbers. You can account for every expense that you anticipate and show on paper a clear plan for running and managing your show. It's a professional presentation that finds favor with the money types who man the desks in the front office, because it displays accountability and thoughtfulness.

If you do it right, it's hard to refute and helps you justify the money you need to do the job you want to do. If Production doesn't have the money you feel you need and can justify, then they might have to agree to scale back on some of their requirements.

One last budget word. In the old days we had what we called "dash numbered account budgets." Here's how they worked. Every studio has its own master show budget forms wherein every department had a number; Wardrobe might be #28... so, CAST RENTALS would be 28 with dash one (28-1), BACKGROUND RENTALS, 28-2, CAST PURCHASES, 28-3, MANUFACTURE, 28-4 and so on. Every expense was coded behind a dash number, and you wrote in your budget dollars like individual bank accounts. As you spent money in any one area, you balanced it against the amount in the corresponding dash numbered account; that way, you always knew where you were budget-wise, and if you had to rob Peter to pay Paul you could balance that too. Nowadays, dash numbered account budgets are rarely used because companies prefer lump sum, all-in-one department budgets.

When hired on a new show and presented with an overall budget amount, always ask, "What does this cover?" If the answer is

"Everything," then develop your own figures anyway. I've never heard of anyone having too much money in their budget, but sometimes the money really is not there. If you back out the hard costs first — rentals, cleaning, supplies, you might find that you have no money for labor. My advice would always be: never take a show that can't afford you. You won't be able to do your best work and it could turn into a production by crisis; pressuring you into the temptation of not paying a vendor or even trying to get friends to help you for little or no money. No matter, you'll be over budget anyway and lose friends and vendors too. And your reputation will suffer, period.

But never say never. Sometimes there's something about some low-budget idea that makes you want to try. An opportunity, a story well articulated, a location adventure, a friend's dream. In those cases, dive in, do your best, have fun, sharpen your skills, eat the challenge and all its problems with gusto. There's nothing like a filmmaking adventure full of hard work and hopefulness. But, if you choose to accept the conditions at the outset, you have no cause to get disgruntled if it doesn't pan out.

One last word. NEVER, NEVER, NEVER, use YOUR MONEY, YOUR CHECKS, or YOUR CREDIT CARDS to finance department requirements, unless you're under a "contractor's" contract and plan to bill the company as a regular part of your business.

Again, please don't make the mistake of underestimating on purpose just to make your budget look better. If you do, you'll be cheating yourself. In the end, you will need the money anyway, at which time you'll look foolish for not knowing your department's REAL requirements ahead of time, and the problem caused to Production will be greater because they will be asked to give you money over-budget instead of planning for it in the beginning. With small film budgets that are borrowed, any late, additional money is the most expensive money they can get and they don't like to do it.

PADDING

This word has gotten a bad name. Building a financial "pad" into your budget is acceptable, although line producers hate the idea. They hate it because THEY pad the show budget against cost over-runs, and they don't want you to do the same thing. In making out any budget, there will be things that you don't anticipate. Adding a little padding to cushion you against additional requirements, cost overruns or future budget cuts is prudent. You are not "hiding" money in your budget; you are estimating on the high side whenever possible, in order to be able to absorb escalating demands or prices later; it's called a "contingency fund."

After you prepare budgets a few times and compare what you spent with what you thought you'd spend, you'll feel right at home doing the breakdowns and plugging in the numbers. You'll also realize that this paper groundwork is a foundation you'll need time after time to have a successful department. Just think of everything you can, assign a reasonable price, and add it up.

A REAL BUDGET STORY

As I write this story, I'm supervising Gods and Generals, *a Civil War epic expected to be in theatres in 2002. I have over a million-dollar budget in these four categories: Rentals, Manufacture, Purchase, and Labor.*

The labor part was structured around using local labor (we're on location in South Carolina) with four people from Hollywood. Four weeks from shooting, I wanted to hire a fifth man because I could not find the experienced help I need here. The producer was resisting because that hiring would put me over my Labor budget.

The solution: Crunch numbers.

I demonstrated that the savings incurred by our package at Western Costume plus our renting rather than making costumes saved close to $100,000 on the accumulated budget. Applying that money to the Labor side, I got my fifth man and had money to spare.

The lesson: Learn to do the math.

Examples of budget and breakdown pages.

SCRIPT CHRONOLOGY.   ①

① SEQUENCE   PG. 1-7   SCNS. 1-3

EXT. JUNGLE D. VIETNAM- 1968

REILANDER (W/ 181 PATCH)
CORBETT
SANDERS
BUELL
DOERR (MEDIC)
ROTH (1ST. SGT)
BVOMBERG (NEW GUY)
RICHARDS
HETHERLY
LEMANSKI
PAILEY   (CAPT. CADRE- 'TIGER STRIPES')

COMBAT COMPANY IN FIELD.- DIRTY/TORN.

+ 20-30 EXTRA SOLDIERS.

② EXT SURVIVAL SCHOOL-HQ-DAY   (SCN #4 EST.)

HUELETTE

WALKS CAMP- 40-50 B.G. EXTRAS /CLEAN.

INT. SURVIVAL SCHOOL HQ.-DAY   (SCN #5.)

HUELETTE (SP-4)
FALZAN (SP-4)
ONETO (SFC)

JOKE ABOUT PET MONKEY (TO WEAR FATIGUES)
W/ "SWADEBECK" NAME TAG.

HUELETTE ASKS FOR NEW ASSIGNMENT.

③ EXT BOTTOM BURNED OUT HILL   SCN #6

REILANDER (COVERED W/BLOOD)
BVOMBERG (SHOT)
BIG SOLDIER (SHOT)
24 B.G. EXTRA SOLDIERS
SOLDIERS ASSAULT HILL.

Script Chronology

COSTUME CROSSPLOT	SET NAME	JUNGLE	BASE CAMP	H.Q.
INT/EXT		E	E	E
D/N		/	/	/
SCN #S		1-3	4	6
CAST				
1 REILANDER		/		
2 HUELETTE		/	/	
3 CORBETTE		/		
4 SANDERS		/		
5 BUELL		/		
6 DOERR (MEDIC)		/		
7 ROTH (1ST. SGT)		/		
8 BYOMBERG		/		
9 RICHARDS		/		
10 HETHERLY		/		
11 PAILEY (CADRE)		/		
12 FALZAN (SP.4)			/	
13 ONETO (SFC)			/	
14				
15				
16				
17				
18				
19				
20				
21				
22				
23				
24				
25				
ATMOS/STUNTS		30	30	
26				
27				
28				
29				
30				
SCENE ACTION.		INTRO	EST. MONKEY	

Costume Crossplot

COSTUME FOR REILANDER.

Change	Scene Nos.	Set	Description
1.	1-3	EXT JUNGLE D.	COMBAT FATIGUES DIRTY-TORN.
	6-7	EXT HILL-BATTLE D.	
	8-9	MEDEVAC AREA D.	*BLOOD.
	10-11-12-14-15	INT. CHOPPER D.	
	16	BASE CAMP D.	
	17-18	BARRACKS D.	TPL'S THIS CHANGE.
2.	19-	LATRINE D.	NEW. FATIGUES. -CUTS OFF NAME-
	22-25-26	1. H.Q. D.	
	28	1. SURVIVAL SCHOOL D.	
	29	PARADE GROUND D.	
	30	BARRACKS D.	
	31	1. SUPPLY HUT. D.	(ISSUED TIGER STRIPES)
3.	34	EXT. SURVIVAL SCH. D.	(NEW 'TIGER STRIPES') -NO NAME OR PATCHES
	35	1. MESS HALL N.	
	36	E. " " N.	
	38	1. E.M. CLUB. N.	
	40	E. E.M. CLUB. N.	
3A.	41.	1. BARRACKS N.	HALF DRESSED-RUNS OUT TO BUNKER.
	42.	E. " N.	
			T'SHIRT-PANTS-BOOTS-ONLY
3B	45-47-49	E. SURVIVAL SCH D.	FULL TIGERSTRIPES. W/All TAGS AND PATCHES SEWN ON
	51	1. MESS HALL D.	
	53	E. SURVIVAL SCH. D.	
	55	1. BASE ADMIN. D.	
	57.	1/E SURVIVAL SCH D.	

Actor Change Sheet

BUDGET TOP SHEET.

PAGE	# 1	B.D.U. JUNGLE	$	13,755
"	# 2	B.D.U. NEW GUYS	$	3,050
"	# 3	CAST.	$	3,450
"	# 4	CADRE	$	5,390
"	# 5	U.S. ARMY NURSE	$	8,700
"	# 6	MISC.	$	1,560
"	# 7	RED CROSS GIRLS	$	2,580
"	# 8	MALE CIVS.	$	2,010
"	# 9	S. VIET CIVS - MEN	$	1,675
"	# 10	S. VIET WOMEN	$	1,575
"	# 11	CHOPPER PILOTS	$	660
"	# 12	V.C. SOLDIERS	$	1,905
"	# 13	N.V.A. SOLDIERS	$	1,050

TOTAL RENT/PURCH $ 52,340

15 'E' CONTAINERS @ 50 = $ 750

ALLOW $2000 COSTUME-
IN-HOUSE LABOR $ 2000

EXP. SUPPLIES $ 3,000

CLEANING/DYING $ 2000

LOCATION LABOR $ 3,000

DEPT TOTAL LESS LABOR $ 63,090

Budget Top Sheet

41

Western Costume Company

Order Request

1.

Purch shirts
pants.

PRODUCTION CO.		DATE 8-31
SHOW NAME LESSONS LEARNED		DATE NEEDED
CONTACT		PO #
PHONE		FAX NUMBER

TYPE OF COSTUME
U.S. ARMY - INFANTRY - VIETNAM 1968 COMBAT COMPANY IN FIELD / AGED!

Amt	Consisting Of	In Stock	Unit Rental	Purch MO	Unit Cost	Total Cost	Total Rental
60	HELMET		10				600
60	LINER		15				900
60	HELMET COVER		10				600
60	CAMO BAND		5				300
150	'T' SHIRT, O.G.		7				1050
50	JUNGLE JACKET (mix) 4P		50				2500
50	PANT TO MATCH (CARGO)		50				2500
50	BELTS - PLIC WEB W/BRASS BUCK.		10				500
100	SHOULDER PATCHES T.B.D. - SUBD			100			
50	BOOTS - JUNGLE - PANAMA TRED.		35				1750
50	HAT, BOONIE O.G.		25				1250
65	SET PIN ON RANK ASST. (3 EACH)		7				455
50	'U.S. ARMY' FLASHES SUBD.		3				150
50	NAME STRIPS - SUBD.		3				150
150	PR. BOOT SOX · O.G.		7				1050
				@ 237			
							13,755

Order Request Form

CHAPTER THREE

COSTUME DESIGN

I'd like to tell a little about the history of "star fittings," and mention a costume designer that just about everyone has heard of: Edith Head.

Back in the roaring twenties, costumes were designed by men. These were designers who came from the world of stage, opera, and silent films. The costumes were, almost always, somewhat over the top, flamboyant.

Edith started in the thirties, with the rise of sound and big studio productions with big studio stars.

Edith helped invent the concept of the "star wardrobe" — merging fashion, contemporary clothes, and costume fantasy to make a star look great on film. By her own admission she was the "queen of camouflage." She would assess everyone the same way in the fitting room: She emphasized good points and took attention away from any awkward points; and she did it all with the simplest of lines. She designed a lot of classic clothes and set the standard. This is the point of the tailor's fitting, to adjust the clothes so that they flatter the star whenever possible with the cut and fit.

Okay, well that's over. Let's get to the part that you most likely bought the book for in the first place, COSTUME DESIGN.

I was talking with another costume designer the other day and he said something that really got me. He said "I don't believe that anyone in this business knows what we do on a show." Actually, that might not be far from the truth.

Of course everyone knows in the broad sense that the costume designer designs clothes... right? Runs the wardrobe department on a show? Makes everything look right? Spends money?

Maybe first we should look at what the job does require, that is, what the production company will be hiring you for and what they will be expecting you to do.

Let's start with a couple of definitions:

DESIGNER
- Creates and works out the details of....
- Makes a pattern or sketch of....

ILLUSTRATOR
- Explains by example.
- Provides pictures or figures....

In Hollywood, costume designers are represented by the Costume Designers Guild, Local #892. To reach them for information, call: (818) 905-1557. Here is what they have to say about the job requirements (the following is paraphrased from their contract):

A. A costume designer is an employee who renders services by creating and designing costumes for principal players and others in any motion picture or television series.

B. In addition to creating and designing, a costume designer may be assigned the supervision of all aspects of costuming a show, including shopping and the selection of stock costumes.

C. A costume designer's duties include the sketching of costumes for the purposes of creating a costume which will be custom-made (made to order) from that sketch.

They go on to say:
Some of the duties of a costume designer are:

A. Attend preproduction and production meetings.

B. Interface with producers, directors, and actors.

C. Have knowledge of script breakdown.

    1. Script analysis and character delineation & progression.

    2. Define special requirements of script as it pertains to costumes.

    3. Preliminary budget.

D. Research.

    1. Translate a one-dimension drawing or photograph into a three-dimensional costume.

E. Creative Development.

    1. Design concept.

    2. Meet with actor, producer, director.

    3. Determine which garments should be made and which should be selected from existing garments.

    4. Sketching.

    5. Collaborate with production team.

F. Realizing the design.

    1. Ability to explain to workroom how costume is to be constructed.

    2. Knowledge of appropriate fabrics.

    3. Follow the creation of the costume from inception to completion.

  G. Preside over fittings.

    1. Communicate design to cutter/fitter and staff.

  H. During film production:

    1. Must be present to establish the look of the character.

    2. Must be present to change the look of the character if there is a conflict on the set.

    3. Maintain the integrity of the look of the show.

    4. Create looks for day and featured players.

    5. Make decisions for the next day's filming.

    6. Keep abreast of script changes.

As costume designer, your job will be twofold: be responsible for the running of the department, and provide for the costumes for the actors and background with a sense of style. The last part, "with a sense of style," is the part that interests most people, and the part that causes all the agony and all the ecstasy.

Where do you start?

You've read the script. Now you have to do a little noodling with a pencil.

Ask yourself a few questions: What kind of piece is it? Drama, comedy, action? What period is it? Is it an outdoor or indoor piece, or a little of each? What kind of characters are there? What kind of action is there? What kind of mood is it? WHAT IS THE STORY?

These questions are important because the correct answers will lead you in the right direction in your costume selection.

Right here let me introduce you to two very different styles of costuming. I call them, "documentary" and "Kabuki."

The documentary approach is obvious from the name and it's the safest because it's the most recognizable. You find out what was worn and reproduce it. Now that's never as easy as it sounds, but you always know what you're doing because of the historical research.

The Kabuki way is more exciting, but if done wrong it can be a disaster. The theory behind Kabuki is that, as you are doing something which never existed before anyway, why attempt to be literal? As the writer created a new reality through this drama, it is fitting that the visual presentation be free to illustrate that drama in a new way. In other words, create your own reality — and if it's true to the drama, no one will question its correctness. This works for specific characters within a film also.

Actually a third way, the middle way (and perhaps the way most of us work) is a synthesis of those two: staying loosely within a historical framework while creating a visual that incorporates dramatic symbolism. Let's explore this a little.

You have to start developing a *style*: some self-imposed rules that will help guide your selection process based on what you want to accomplish. Go back to your graph-paper breakdown. You will see that the show takes place in location after location, through time. Your main characters will travel from one end of the script to the other, through a series of scenes and sets, each one having secondary characters and background atmosphere, a mood, and a time, living out the story. Your job is to ILLUSTRATE the drama with costumes so that the audience will accept the story via the visual construct. The costumes must support the dramatic premise of the piece in terms of their realism, integrity and artfulness, and aid the actors by supporting and distinguishing their characters through their look.

The show itself will tell you what it calls for... all the clues are there.

When I went to film school at Pasadena Art Center, our instructor gave me a piece of advice that has proved itself time after time. It goes like this: When, as a designer, someone tells you, "I want this picture to look as real as possible," they most likely don't mean it — not in the historical sense anyway. What they actually mean is, "I want this picture to be ACCEPTABLE as real." Which means, they want a good, professional illustration, not a high school play. In other words, they want it true to character, but not always true to life.

For you, determining the level of illustration is the VERY FIRST STEP on the right track or the wrong track.

Metaphysically you can look at it this way: All material existence is only symbolic of the invisible principles that have brought it into being. Symbolism is the root of theatrical costume design. Costumes become metaphors for your characters' character. The clothes reflect the times, action, station, conditions, and even inner turmoil of your screen characters, while the background costumes create the world that your main characters populate.

The question is, how do you create an effective illustration? First, look at how others have done it.

See as many films as you can — new ones, old ones, silent ones, foreign ones. See where the characters feel right and where the characters feel wrong, where the background seems authentic or where it's hokey.

Most films are populated with stock characters, that is, characters that we might meet in everyday life or everyday film life: the doctor, judge, sheriff, hooker, housewife, good guy, bad guy, love interest, bum, bartender, etc.

We've seen them so many times that these characters have become stereotypes. We recognize them at a glance. They have a look all their own, and unless you're playing against type for a reason, it may be better to follow the traditional lead and try and create characters that are recognizable but unique to your story.

This is truly where your job becomes exciting and challenging. You are to use the same general tools that have been used before... on the same types of characters that everyone's seen before... and come up with something that will stand alone as yours... while being at once understandable to an audience, supporting the dramatic premise, and helping the actors fashion the characters.

It's a lot, but isn't as hard as it might seem. Everything that goes in front of the camera represents a series of selections, and every selection is done with a reason in mind. When you break down the script as a designer (illustrator), you're discovering and developing the REASONS that will enable you to make the BEST selections. Your reasons will become more refined as you develop more information (color theory, historical knowledge, the language of symbolism) and your selections will also become more refined.

When you read a script you can picture it. Maybe the picture is a little foggy, a little unclear in detail. What you need to do is organize your thoughts, analyze the requirements, and find out what's available.

The first place to start might be the question: Why do people wear clothes?

Historically, the first use of clothing was for protection from the weather, then war. No one can say where or when adornment started, but grave excavations have produced beads and small disks that go back tens of thousands of years.

Egyptians were weaving linen and making gold jewelry six thousand years ago, and tribe people from the China steppes were wearing decorated felted clothing two thousand years before that. The ten-thousand-year-old "Ice Man," found frozen in the Italian Alps, was wearing a recognizable, fitted, leather shirt and pants with woven fiber sandals; and mummies from the Andes have been found wrapped in woven woolen blankets with geometric designs.

Other reasons for clothing: a display or reflection of rank (position); class (wealth); culture (ethnic, social, moral); and for beauty's sake, to feel and/or be attractive (even in a countercultural sense).

The *reasons* don't change, but the clothing does — according to period, location, culture, and conditions.

If you have to do a story about ancient China, a culture about which you may know nothing... with a little research into styles and fabric, you know that the king will be fancier than the farmer. Ancient Egypt? The dancing girl will have less on than the merchant's wife, and so it goes.

Certain recognizable images of character appear, the self-absorbed rich guy, the vain "other woman." We know the types, the characters, we know how they would *see themselves*, how they would express themselves with clothing. The fun part is creating them anew, or re-creating with symbolism in a fresh way, to tell your story uniquely. In other words, we can grasp their self-image as they are portrayed in the screenplay... but what, actually, would they wear?

Go to visual research (this includes modern fashion).

When researching a period (or "look") there are really only four things to look for:

- Silhouette
- Line (actual seams and cut)
- Detail (of construction, including fabric and jewelry)
- Color

Most periods are recognizable by their silhouette — so most people familiar with period clothes can spot the major changes by the size of the dress or length of the coat. Designing a futuristic show can also start with a concept of silhouette. What best reflects the character or conditions? Sleek, heavy, layered? A lightly covered body or one shrouded to the point of concealment?

Within the silhouette is the line and detail. Is it draped or fitted, double- or single-breasted? Does it have bound edges? What's the fabric like?

If characters are tedious, so might be the print of their tie or dress. List the character traits of your cast, then translate them, symbolically, into costume — using cut, fabric, and color.

This is both the creative and dangerous part. In some scripts, a wild, clearly fantasy world is the background. In these cases you are free to invent a look that has nothing to do with reality and everything to do with symbols. But what about shows that are set in the past? Westerns or period dramas? Contemporary films? Audience members have seen things like this before and have preconceived ideas about what these films should look like. In these films you have to walk a fine line, making the costumes realistic enough to be accepted and not distracting, while using your skills at illustration to highlight or underline characters and dramatic situations — sometimes with special bits of wardrobe, sometimes with color. It all goes back to the same thing. What kind of illustration best fits the story?

With regard to the shape of the clothes, it all starts with the cutting. Where are the control darts? How tight is the arm hole? Period clothes arrive at their distinctiveness by their cut (and fabric), so you have to do some studying as to the historical progression of clothing. Remember, the more you choose to compromise the cut of period costumes for the sake of actors' comfort or as a concession to modern fashion sensibilities, the farther you will get from the look of the period.

For fabric, you have many choices, and you can break them down into categories, which will make the selection process easier. Let's start with the two easiest to recognize: LIGHT ABSORBENT and LIGHT REFLECTIVE. Most natural fabrics are light absorbent except for silk and, to a degree, polished cotton and linen. Most man-made fabrics are light reflective — rayon, nylon, satin, and polyester. Light reflective materials can look elegant — as in a women in a silk dress in a room full of black tuxedos — or, because of its shine, can look cheap if overused. For period clothing, here are good guidelines to follow: the lower class wears light absorbent (dull), the upper class wears light reflective (silks with gold or silver and fur trim). The gangster wears a shiny silk suit, the sober judge wears a gray wool matte-finish, and the wife wears a simple black dress. While the hooker is obvious in gold lamé shorts and vinyl boots, the simple cowboy wears a dirt-colored vest, and the gambler wears silk brocade.

Rule of thumb: the more honest and down-to-earth, the more light absorbent. The more wealthy or posturing as wealthy, the more light reflective.

Another consideration that will help you make decisions about the costumes will be color. Overall color and specific color. How will you use it?

Again, while there are hundreds of hues, and shades and tones thereof, there are only two color schemes possible: COMPLEMENTARY and ANALOGOUS. Get yourself a color wheel at an art store. The way a color wheel is arranged makes it easy to understand. Analogous color harmonies are colors that sit next to each other on the wheel and are more sympathetic to each other, while complementary harmonies are directly across the wheel from each other and offer more contrast.

In addition to colors you also have black and white. How to best use them depends on the specific nature of your project and the drama you're going to try to illustrate.

First, a few more terms:

The word *monochromatic* is frequently used and misused in production meetings by production designers and others. A monochromatic color scheme means a single color with various tonal values. In other words, eight shades of oatmeal.

My experience is that a lot of production designers are afraid of color overuse in the finished film or afraid that the costume person isn't capable of using color with restraint, so they ask for monochromatic. But is that what they really want?

In the seventies, when I first started hearing that term, some Westerns were done in monochrome, that is, everything was over-dyed with sepia and became values of brown.

Today, when I hear that term, it usually means that a full-color palette is acceptable if the various colors are mitigated and sympathetic in tone, with no "hot" color to distract the eye.

The answer here is over-dying two attractive but muted color combinations. Period shows, Westerns, and dark dramas can be darker and more single-value, but still have a full-color palette.

The necessity and importance of color requires that you learn color terms and usage from art instruction books on color theory. This is because art books use and explain the standard terms; and they will be the same terms that the production designer will know. Remember, everything you do is going to be filmed and displayed much like a "moving painting." The director of photography (DP), the production designer, the key electrician, the set painters and scenic artists — they all think and work with this in mind, so you should too.

You should learn to think about color in percentage values. White is "zero" while black is "one hundred." Now, where does your color fall? If I said "Let's keep all our color around fifty percent or darker," would you understand? The production designer would. If you were told, "Over-dye everything with tan; that will mute the colors and bring them into the same range," would you understand?

What changes color is *value*. Is it light or dark? *Intensity* is the purity or strength of a color. Then there's *tone*: is it warm or cool? *Shade* and *tint* refer to the use of white or black to move a hue up or down the tonal scale.

You might also want to study painters of the two color schools: Colorist and Tonalist. The basic difference is: both schools felt that the impact of a painting rested in the tension created by contrast. Tonalists did it with subtle palettes, using tones and values of largely analogous schemes; colorists did it by using primary palettes of bright colors, often with complementary schemes.

With color usage rules and film sensibilities in mind, a "safe" costume pull might start at monochromatic (medium analogous) neutral and natural; that is, with medium-brown (warm) or gray (cool) as a general background color. You could include off-whites (tan for warm, or gray for cool) and dark browns (warm) or dark blues (cool) set off with black. The next colors to introduce might be: dark purple, dull reds, dark earthy greens and "dirty" or dark yellows and oranges. Even with a restricted palette you can get "life" out of your characters. You can use analogous colors in the background costumes and complementary schemes on the main characters.

My mother once told me, "If you want to do a beautiful period show, go look at the colors at the produce counter; and if you're doing a musical, look in a flower shop." It's true. If the subject of your project is happy, sunny, and innocent, then the colors have to support it. If your mood or character is dark and cold, then the colors have to reflect that. If your subject is ancient or ethnic then the colors have to be natural. If modern, the dye color should be harder, more aniline.

To sum it up so far: The cut is historical and reflects the period; the fabric is textural and reflects the status; the color is emotional and reflects the mood.

Look at each element, character and background, separately. Imagine if a book were written about this character or scene, and you had the job of illustrating the book cover so that one look told everything, what would that illustration look like?

Again, you have to conceive of yourself as an artist, whose job it is to illustrate a character, a drama, a mood, a period, a social condition. Your tools are: period references, hanging stock, the workroom, fabric, dye, trimmings, department organization, imagination and artistic knowledge... and, of course, some money from the producer.

Everything you do will be photographed on film, so it might be good to talk a little about the process of photography and what effect it has on the clothes. And before you can photograph anything you have to have light on it. It's this essential element, the lighting, that is important to understand, because it, too, has to do with the mood of the drama.

For anything recorded on film, there are only four "lighting plots" possible. They are: *high key/high contrast, high key/low contrast, low key/high contrast, and low key/low contrast.*

HIGH KEY/HIGH CONTRAST

The "key" light is the main light, lighting the set. A HIGH KEY light might be the sun. *Contrast* means the amount of shadow or the balance of light between highlight and shadow. So HIGH KEY/HIGH CONTRAST might be natural sunlight with no bounce or secondary light to soften the shadows. The overall light is hot and hard, while the shadows are deep. This might be the lighting used on a Western, or something on the desert or at sea, very natural-looking. Highlights tend to be very hot, causing whites and light colors to "burn out." Pastels look weak, so medium and dark colors work the best. This kind of lighting can also burn out aging and have the effect of "cleaning" the clothes on screen.

I once had to make clothes for Apache Indians. They wore off-white garments in a Mexican peon style with breechclouts and high moccasins. We made the outfits in off-white muslin, kind of a dirty white. They looked fine. We took them outside in the bright sunshine. Wow! They sparkled white. So we over-dyed them with Rit. I wanted them to "read" white on camera but not glare... out of the dryer they looked almost too brown... but outside, TOO BRIGHT AGAIN! We finally put about three dye washes on them. To the eye, they were tan, but in the sun, they were slightly off-white, just right.

HIGH KEY/LOW CONTRAST

This would be a bright light overall, with a lot of fill light to take out the shadows... a musical, comedy, or sitcom. With the perfect artificial lighting balance, colors of a larger spectrum can be used, because there won't be any hot highlights or color lost in shadow. The effect is almost like "abstract painting" with pure colors.

LOW KEY/HIGH CONTRAST

Overall this lighting is dim. It can have very bright spot lighting, but with lots of shadows. This works for a moody piece, film noir, horror. If an overall darkness is required, use medium to dark clothing in the cool tones. Whites will look strong and should be dyed down. Jewel tones will look rich; whites, if used, will look sharp; blacks are a great anchor. Subtle prints are good to break up color masses.

LOW KEY/LOW CONTRAST

Overall this look is dim, soft, and even, without the dark shadows or blinding highlights. This one's good for a love story on the Irish coast in the fog. Everything looks great here.

Something you have to be conscious of is that the picture you see on a television screen is made up of electronic signals. These pixels are like a honeycomb of tiny squares, each square getting information about what color it's supposed to be. If you use a fabric with a tight pattern, especially black-and-white check, the honeycomb squares can't read the moving print fast enough to change, so they get confused and start switching back and forth between black and white... this is called strobing, and it's distracting to the viewer.

Have you ever looked at a crowd of people and seen someone who seemed so out of place that you said to yourself, "If I dressed someone that way they'd fire me"? Well, I have. The thing is, we are all used to seeing the imperfections that compose reality. The more "perfect" something looks, the more false or unnatural it will seem. A musical, far removed from reality, looks the most false or perfect; while a war film or Western, posing as "real drama" is full of facial hair and character wardrobe.

While I like to draw and even paint as a hobby, costume sketches often scared the heck out of me. Why? Well, I always had a hard time figuring out WHO the sketch was for — e.g., if the sketch were for the tailor then it should show the cut; if for the producer, director, actor, perhaps more concept.

My first film as costume designer (*The Wind and the Lion*, 1975) took me to Spain, where I set up shop at a Spanish costume house. I wanted to do well, to create something really wonderful. I agonized over dresses for the leading lady. I poured over period photos, drawings, paintings. I went back to my hotel room every night to draw and redraw her dress. It never looked right; either the dress was wrong or the drawing was stiff. Finally I got it, both the drawing and the dress were right, at least it was as good as I was going to do. I rushed to show it to the production designer and the director. They loved it. I felt great. I went back to the Spanish costume house workroom. The head cutter-fitter was a middle-aged Spanish woman, thin, droopy eyelashes, a cigarette always at the corner of her mouth. I put my sketch on her cutting table. "This," I announced, "is the dress you'll be making for Miss so-and-so." She eyed the sketch a moment, took a long puff and answered, "Beautiful darling, how's the back cut?" I looked at my sketch, the one I had poured so many hours into... I hadn't the faintest idea about the back... I felt really dumb.

You see what I mean. But if you make the sketch too workroom-oriented, showing every seam and panel, it looks too stiff. If it's for the director, then maybe it should be more concept, i.e., major lines and color. If it's for the actor... should it look like that person? Should it be one of those impossibly long-legged sketches from fashion magazines which have a lot of style but tend to look affected and unreal? How does one pick a rendering style that satisfies everyone? The solution is to make more than one sketch.

First, do a CONCEPT drawing for the director, producer, production designer, showing how you FEEL about the clothes in general: loose, tight, baggy, flowing, color, texture — all draped onto a reasonably realistic, but unrecognizable, human body shape, in loose color on board. The second rendering, a line drawing intended for the workroom, should explain your ideas in more detail, as more blueprint than art. Last, do a "finished" sketch. Remember, it might be a good idea to do a concept sketch first, swatch the material, *then* do the finished sketch. A finished drawing is only a drawing; it's not a good idea to sell a concept with a beautiful idea on paper, then have to try to find whether the right material actually exists.

About drawing: I believe that *anyone* with a desire to draw, can get good with practice. As far as the human figure goes, there are lots of resources to copy from, and copy you should, over and over, from photos or life, until you "catch the line" that we all recognize as human. It gets easier with time.

If you start a period show, you may want to sit down with a ream of 8½" x 11" paper and some research books. Start copying every costume illustration you think fits with what you are doing. Soon, you will develop a good feeling for what lines are repeated over and over.

Doing this before you sit down to sketch for cast costumes gives you the familiarity with the period that will put confidence in your sketches and give you a knowledge and feeling for things like detail and trim, which will help you design more realistic clothing. If you're uncertain or insecure with paint, I would start with color pencils, a little at a time. Get going in the right direction. When the drawing starts to look more firm start adding color with paint in broad areas. I favor acrylics and have never developed any confidence with watercolor, but I've seen and admired others who could render beautiful costume sketches with watercolor or gouache.

Remember, any technique or combination of mediums that expresses your idea to others is fair. There are no rules except that your rendering should be readable, expressive, and help sell your ideas.

I have included in this book some sketches of my own. My drawing style has changed over the years from show to show. Some of the work was done in the safety of my studio at home; some on hastily built drawing boards on location with the workroom waiting; some are concept sketches or quick sketches; some are more complete; but I include a variety to show you the possibilities (color sketches in the middle of the book, B/W sketches in the Appendix).

Don't forget, if all else fails, there are many great costume illustrators registered with the Costume Designers Guild, people who help designers that are too busy or don't feel that they want do the renderings themselves.

MAKING CLOTHES
There are only three ways to make clothes:

1. Have them made at a costume house that is set up for manufacture with its own workroom.

2. Find outside sewing contractors or "cut and sew" places, shopping the fabric yourself.

3. Set up your own workroom.

Each method has its advantages and disadvantages. There's a time and place for each, so let's take them one at a time.

THE COSTUME HOUSE Most costume houses have in-house tailor shops where they do their own alterations and light manufacture. I say "light" manufacture because costume houses aren't set up for mass production work, but rather for individual garment construction. If you want to make suits or dresses for the leading cast this might be a good option. Prices can vary but because they are all union shops, they pay decent wages and are sometimes more expensive than you would think. This might be offset by the fact that they usually have fabric sources and supplies on the premises, and that the workroom help is as good as you will find anywhere, and often better than most places. These are professional costume and clothing makers with years of experience, and the costume house will stand behind their work. They are used to working with both designers and stars, and are very conscious of deadlines, workmanship, and the fact that what they do will be photographed for the big screen."

The costume houses have access to, and first-hand knowledge of, many workroom people, which takes the guesswork out of hiring for you. Overall, costume house manufacture, or what's called *M.O. work* ("made-to-order") is very dependable. But it's still a good idea to get estimates first.

FARMING IT OUT This option usually is considered when you're faced with building great numbers of "alike" things, armies for example. This entails finding a sewing contractor or a cut and sew business that will make room in its production schedule to help you. The burden for design, direction, samples, and materials is all on you — and if their quality control is sloppy, it doesn't matter, you still pay for it. You may find problems with lack of seam allowance, grading to larger or smaller sizes, finished work that is measured "seam to seam" rather than with an allowance for fit, and the ever-present "It won't be ready for another week." That being said, however, the good news is that there are many good contractors out there who will help you if you can afford the time to find them.

In the end, though, it might be better to let a costume house accomplish this type of work for you, because they have done it before, have their own favorite contractors, and understand the steps in making and finishing large manufacture orders. You will, of course, pay for their participation, but that is almost always offset by the dependability factor.

DO IT YOURSELF   On shows where you have a shortfall of rentable stock and a large amount of diverse items to find, this choice might make the most sense.

Let's say that you have a Western to do, and you realize that you need sets of triple shirts or dresses that you can't find; or you have to do a tribe of Indians that doesn't exist on the rack. You may be working on a period piece where the available stock is thin. The amount of necessary items needed is large, with a lot of variety. To expect a costume house to do the work might be unreasonable due to their facility space, their own work schedule, or the price.

Outside commercial sewing contractors, while good at mass production, might not be able to respond to the variety of cutting on small, individual amounts within your large order, and would probably not be able to offer you the full-time access you would need in order to oversee the work or its finishing.

Setting up a workroom (discussed somewhat in the budget section), is a very deliberate operation that takes experience and good management. As always, time and money are the enemies. If you're going to try this, hire the best, most experienced supervisor that you can to work out the four-wall facility details.

When it comes to clothing manufacture, it all starts with the cutter-fitter; this is the person whose knowledge, skill, and experience will determine the look and fit of the finished garment. From the cutter-fitter, the work will pass down through the "Table Lady" to the finishing tailors.

The best cutter-fitters in the world are in the motion picture industry. On the west coast they are represented by the Costumers Local #705, (323) 851-0220. They are the ones that have worked in every period. Most outside cutters have only worked in limited areas: wedding gowns, fashion, or ready-to-wear. While they are good at what they do, usually they don't have the experience that Hollywood cutters have with regard to the variety of clothing or knowing about the end result of costumes worn on the screen. Also, most outside cutters use the "block" pattern method for arriving at patterns; while block pattern cutting is good for modern clothing, it's not the way that period clothes were cut, so rendering a period coat or dress without the correct draping will result in a garment that isn't quite right.

If you are on a union show, your manufacture labor has to be union. Many a designer has succumbed to the temptation to hire someone they know that is non-union only to pay a fine later; check with Local #705 for details.

Setting yourself up to run a workroom is challenging but rewarding. Be sure to give it a lot of thought and work it out on paper first.

Consider: What are we going to build? How much space will it take and how long will I need that space? Where will that space be and how much will it cost? What kind of shop equipment will be required, and where will it come from? What kind of labor will be needed in terms of experience and expertise, and what will that cost? What will have to be done in order to meet the production schedule?

It's hard work and takes a lot of planning but you can do it. You probably won't have to work very long as a designer before you want to (or have to) try it.

The only secret: get the best help you can, and enough of it!

One last thing: If you're doing it yourself, remember, send that material out first to be hot-washed to take out the shrinkage before you start to cut anything!

FITTING THE ACTOR   There are two kinds of fittings: the one that happens when making clothes, and the one that happens after the costumes are assembled and the actor comes in to try on all the costume changes for the project. The first is a natural outgrowth of the tailor shop process. The clothes are being made, the actor has to put them on and see how they fit... adjustments are made, the clothes go back to the shop and the actor goes home.

61

In the thirties, the era of the studio system, there was a lot of prep time given, and a reasonable amount of money was available to get the stars on screen. There were legendary partnerships between some designers and stars such as Orry-Kelly and Bette Davis, and Cecil Beaton and Marlene Dietrich. The fifties brought Travilla and Marilyn Monroe, and from the world of fashion, Givenchy and Audrey Hepburn. More recently, there is Bob Mackie and Cher.

To a large degree, these designers were looking to create a fantasy image. Today, films are less glamorous and more "real," so they seem to call for more real-looking clothing. There are, of course, many talented designers working today, too many for me to mention here.

Years ago, Mom (who is from the old school), instructed me on how to go about making dresses for an actress, basing her advice on the studio system in which she had worked for years: "First, do your research, get photos from history books that get you close to the right look, then do a concept sketch and swatch everything. Find a dress in stock that comes close to what you want. Put the sample garment on a dress form and sketch it. Staple the swatches to the sketch. Go to the camera department, have them photograph the drawing and material with the film stock that they're going to shoot the film with, and put the photo with the drawing; then go to the head cutter-fitter, have her do a yardage count on the fabric you want and get it priced. Finally, check with the ladies' wardrobe department supervisor to see if the proper foundation garments exist or have to be made also. Then prepare all the dress change drawings in the same way for a show-and-tell with the producer and director, where you can discuss the look, all the manufacture and its prices."

As beautiful and professional a system as that once was, I know that I've never had the time to even think about doing that much groundwork on things that had to be made (although the steps, as an ideal to aim for, are great to know).

My point is that the business has changed. It's harder now to do the kind of work that those brilliant designers of yesterday did — for a few reasons. First, lack of time and money. Today, all but the biggest features are shot with slim budgets. This means less prep time and less manufacture, which means more reliance on the rental of stock items. Second, stock at costume houses is not replaced with any regularity so you might find that your show, when rented, is a mixture of first and second choices, at least where the background is concerned. That's why limited manufacture and tailor fitting with leading cast members is the most important, because these are the people who will be telling the story, who will have most of the screen time, and who will likely be featured in twenty-foot-high shots. This is the place to spend time and money.

It's a good idea to photograph the fittings with special attention to close-up shots, remembering that when the actor will be filmed, much of it will be in close-up for dialogue. How does that collar, tie, hat, or anything else around the face look? No matter about the great job you did finding and getting all the fantastic-looking clothes for everyone else. If the actor in close-up is ill-fitting, the rest doesn't mean much.

Now let's discuss the second kind of fitting, which comes when the costumes are assembled in your department. This comes after you have selected choices for the changes for each actor, and that actor comes in to see the clothes, sometimes for the first time. Maybe the actor doesn't like them. Maybe the actor wants to wear something else... that's the fitting we want to look at now.

It will happen on every show. All the preliminary discussion about wardrobe, costume changes, and specific character looks will be done with the director, producer, and production designer — everyone except the person who will be asked to wear the actual clothes. What if that person has other ideas?

To be sure, in most cases you will enjoy some contact with the leading actors before the shoot. You should have the opportunity to exchange ideas on their roles and arrive at something you both can live with... and, many actors, seasoned professionals who are cast late, know the futility of demanding too much attention or specific wardrobe. But of course, they all have their own ideas about what they're doing and how best to illustrate it.

I was working at the American Costume Company once. It's a place known for its top-of-the-line period clothes. One day, a designer and two costumers appeared and announced that they would be pulling clothes all week for a "commercial" fitting. They pulled racks and racks of clothes, coats, vests, shirts, hats, and rolled them close to the fitting room. They pulled the clothes by color and texture with no regard for size. Soon the other costumer arrived with three or four racks of clothing rented from other houses.

The big day came. A dozen chairs were set up in a semi-circle. In came the director, producers, script supervisor, unit manager, and agency people. The designer and two wardrobe helpers stood at the ready, and in came two actors... a man and a woman.

"Okay, let's get started..." The next two hours were a mad house. The designer tried to officiate, like a ringmaster, while the two costumers ran, fetched and helped dress the talent. "How about a darker coat?" asked the director. "I don't like that hat," said the script supervisor. Costumers flew, clothes were shown quickly to the designer, actors disappeared into the fitting room, and reappeared redressed. "I don't know, how about something brighter?" "Looks a little too television." Clothes, once organized on racks, began to jumble. Had the clothes been left in the aisles they would have been easier to find. Now they were half in the aisle and half on racks which they couldn't get to or see, and since they hadn't been pulled by size no one knew what was where. One costumer went for a vest, one for a coat... they didn't go together, no one knew what the other one was pulling... color organization disappeared in the rush to satisfy each request. In the end, the actors had changed every five minutes for two hours. The director looked mildly satisfied at having straightened out yet another creative challenge. The costumers were almost in tears and not speaking to each other. The designer was considering a new career.

What I'm going to tell you now is true: In thirty-five years of dressing actors (in the hundreds), I haven't had a dozen outfits changed on the set, and not too many changed at the fittings. Is it because I'm great? Not at all. It's because I was taught a much better system than what I just described — and it works.

Let's say you're on the show you've always dreamed about. You've had all the concept meetings, you have your research, you're ready. How do you set up the actors' fitting so that the clothes YOU like will be the clothes THEY like? Naturally, the actors will want to look "their best," at least as far as their characters are concerned.

By the time the actors start to come in, you have had some weeks of prep. Think of your breakdown sheets, cast and background. I try, in the department, during preparation, to group the clothes together *by set*. That is, I try to hang the costumes together in the order that they will be used by scene. I do this so that I can see them together. So that every group develops its own integrity. Department costumers can also learn the "looks," and costume units can be worked on by group. After all, that's how they're going to appear on screen, and this is as close to a costume rehearsal as you will get.

I then assemble the cast clothing by actor, with a couple of options for each change. I search them out, sort them out, hang them together so I know what change will work where. At this time, if I can't find something for the actor to wear, I try and find samples that are close in cut or style, regardless of size or color. I put these samples in their order, with swatches of the fabric intended for the new manufacture so the actor can see the proposed garments and the tailor can discuss them at the upcoming fitting.

I try to integrate EVERYTHING I know about the character, everything I've felt from reading the script, everything I've seen in research, everything I've heard in meetings, everything I've found or made according to everything I believe as a costume illustrator. I then check the character changes against each other if they appear in the scene together, to be sure they work together and that they express the dramatic intent of the scene and the characters' relationships. At this point it's a good idea to check with the production designer about the specific set colors that will be the background for the costumes. THEN call the actor in for a fitting with the tailor. NO ONE ELSE!

When the actor arrives, I try to be as friendly and relaxed as I can (sometimes this is not easy). I start with the research... show period illustrations and design sketches, explain the concept, show the color chips and swatches. Then we move to the clothes, group by group, set by set. I try to show the actor what will be around, give a sense of scale and atmosphere, a sense of thoroughness. Then on to the clothes for the rest of the cast. This is the good guy, this is the bad guy, this is the leading lady... this is her change when you meet her for the first time... these are your clothes.

It's essential to give the actor a sense of comfort. You want the actor to be at ease in the clothes. Actors want to feel free to be their character, not distracted by worries that they don't look right. They have to both fit in, and stand out simultaneously.

The best way to do this is to show them that they are part of a larger design, and that within that design their costumes have their own attention points. Explain that the costumes create a visual illustration in which the character can relax, take comfort, and be inspired and strengthened.

Now, you and the actor can find the "gags" for the outfits, i.e., things they can personalize. A hat to push around, a handkerchief to mop the forehead, a bag to clutch nervously, things that will help "sell the character" in the scenes to come. Frequently, character costumes are strengthened by "signature" pieces. A signature piece can be anything — a hat, tie, jewelry, scarf, shoulder pads, a color scheme, a tight look or a baggy shirt... something that defines the character and stays the same or repeats, even though other parts of the costumes change. A signature piece says "this is really who the character is" while the rest of the costume changes are a function of time or circumstance.

If an actor walks into a dressing room without the benefit of knowing or trusting you, or knowing what the show will look like, you can't blame the guy for being defensive or wanting something in particular. My experience is that when actors are comfortable with their clothes, they will be your biggest ally. THEN have your show-and-tell time (or "show-and-yell" as it's sometimes called) with the director. You'll find that the actor will sell your clothes to the director, while you stand back and smile.

There's another way to do it that is less self-assertive and more collaborative. Everything stays the same, except, in addition to selecting actors' changes, you select everything you can that might constitute the characters' wardrobe closet. When the actors come in for the fitting, you show them what you like and "the closet," and then you "play"... trying on this and that until you arrive at something that the actor is comfortable with. This is a better way to work with some stars. They are smart people and most of the time know what works for them. The only problem with this style of arriving at costumes is that, if the star has a vision of the character's clothes that is far from the show you have in mind, what do you do? How many other characters' costumes will you have to adjust? Does the color palette still work? This is why I favor constructing a strong sense of design with color and costumes that I can show the actors as each comes in for the first time. I think it's good to establish a "show reality" that makes everyone feel comfortable.

Let's say that you've done all the prep work, selected the costume changes, and when the actor walks in you know at a glance that everything you picked is wrong. Sometimes, no matter how good your design concept, you realize that you hadn't seen the actor before; and now that you can, you know that the clothes are not going to look right on that person. Graciousness and flexibility are the key. If you are surrounded by your whole department, you can undoubtedly find something, at least to get started. Never lose control of your fitting. Apologize. Bring the actor into the process. "I thought this would be good for your character... but now that I see you, I'm not sure. What do you think?" Work together. I believe in these cases that the actors will be impressed enough by your concern, frankness, and willingness to find the right thing, that they will gladly help brainstorm a "character session" with you, and together, you can make something wonderful happen.

Sometimes you will have a first choice... and someone will want another thing, maybe see another dress or tie, and like it better. Some designers are disappointed at not having a first choice accepted. Is the second thing a bad choice? The reality is that anything that an actor chooses comes out of the costume stock that you've already selected, so they're really all your choices. Take heart in this fact and be happy.

The last thing. Sometimes, there are storms at sea. Sometimes, arguments, dissatisfaction, misunderstandings, and insecurities can manifest themselves at the moment of truth known as the fitting, like dark and furious storm clouds. At once you're the happy sailor, confidently piloting your small craft across a calm sea and... hurricane Evil blows in... chaos and destruction, everything is in shambles, the decks are awash with blood. You're back in the fitting room alone, clothes are everywhere, you're trying to remember what everyone was yelling about. If this happens, remember, it was nothing personal. The thing to do NOW is damage control.

Graciousness and flexibility are what's needed most to get under way again. Be heroic, make it happen... everyone will love it and respect you for it.

Once everything is set, a real show-and-tell with the director is a must. In fact, during the beginning phases of preparation I'm always building toward the show-and-tell meeting. The reasons for this are simple. First, to show common courtesy. When hired, we work for Production, so it's our job to give them the show that they want (and sometimes better). Whether or not your view of a costume is at variance with the director's or producer's, you owe them a meeting, showing and explaining all things before shooting, answering questions and working out kinks before you get to the set. Also, a show-and-tell is the professional thing to do. After all, it's a collaboration and this is the time-honored way that things happen before production. Sometimes the clothes are hanging when viewed, or sometimes it's a "dress parade" with one or more actors wearing their changes for Production to see. Another reason the show-and-tell is important is that it gives you personal satisfaction. You've worked hard during prep to accumulate and fit your costumes, so be proud of them, show them off. If you are at variance with Production about a concept or character, nothing will help you more than a confident display of your reasons. This is also a prime opportunity to show off your department. Up until now, your relationship with Production has been mostly in small meetings or on the phone. They've never really seen what you've been doing, and many times don't appreciate the volume of costumes you will have to handle, the size of your shop, or its contribution to the show. All they know is that they have been asked to pay for it. So, now's your time to show them everything: the look of the background, set by set, other cast members, special items, and made items. Show them that you're prepared, and that they will have a great-looking show. Chances are they will come away with a new appreciation for you and your department, and everyone can march into shooting together with confidence and optimism.

A really good show-and-tell will involve the property master. Some prop people won't be as keen as others, but if they're willing and available it's always good to see the costumes with the jewelry, canes, guns, glasses, and other hand props that will help create the characters.

The show-and-tell approach will have dividends later on too, on the set. If everyone has seen and approved of the costumes ahead of time, then there are no surprises. Everyone feels comfortable with what they see and you're much less likely to hear things like; "I didn't know she was going to wear that!" or "I hate this outfit!" or the infamous "I'm not going to wear that!"

As you fill the show's costume requirements, you will, from time to time, find a place for "gag" outfits, which come in two types. There's the "character" gag outfit, which might be the town drunk in a Western. Here's what I mean. Let's say you have that character in your script and don't know what to do to sell the outfit; just putting him in regular clothing wouldn't do it, because he would look like everybody else... you feel you have to do something special, but what? Then you see an old silent comedy (the best repository for character gag outfits ever) and see a drunk come out of a bar. The silent drunk is denoted visually, by his attached shirt collar, loose at one side, sticking up alongside his ear, and, his starched shirt bosom, free and rolled up his front, showing under an open vest. You recognize him immediately and laugh at the cleverness of those long-ago costumers who knew how to make character through the costumes themselves.

In other words, a "gag" character outfit is one that is slightly exaggerated. You make it especially to set a character apart in something other than regular clothes. The end result is that it looks almost real, just a little off-kilter.

I remember an old Western, where the hero, played by Jimmy Stewart, came into a wild mining-town saloon and was met by the town madam, who wore a dress that had enormous, pointed bosoms. She looked ludicrous to the audience, who laughed, but everyone in the film treated her like nothing was out of the ordinary. It gave the movie a bizarre dimension that made it more imaginative and fun.

The second kind of "gag" outfit is one that works because of the script.

On *Goonies* (1985) there was a child character who was an inventor. His inventions were always going a little bit wrong. In one scene, to scare the bad guys, he wore inflatable muscles that puffed him up when he pulled a CO_2 bottle string. We had to make a change for him that would look like the costume he wore in the rest of the film, but it would have to expand on cue. The back of his outfit was made with spandex inserts, and custom-made balloons were attached under his clothing, hooked up to feed lines connected to large bottles of compressed air whose valves were controlled by an effects man. The whole rig was very difficult for the boy to put on and off because of the inside rigging, but in the end, it worked fine.

On *Curse of the Pink Panther* (1983) there were many gags, but the one that I remember having fun with was supposed to be on an airplane. The Inspector (Peter Sellers) walked down the aisle, his watch caught in the turban of an Indian passenger sitting down, and as the Inspector walked away to the bathroom, the turban unwound off the Indian's head. We made a sewn-down turban on a felt hat blank, bringing it up in a dome shape. We then coiled thirty feet of turban wrapping inside the dome with the first couple of wraps on the outside, and it looked great when it unraveled.

My strangest and most interesting job of gag costuming was on a film called *Stitches* (1985). It was a comedy about a bunch of kids in medical school. The end of the movie centered around a student parade where all the kids (about fifty) wore walk-around outfits that simulated body parts. When I read the script, I realized that this job was not going to be accomplished by regular costume people, so I rounded up a crew of makeup effects people, set up shop in a rented industrial unit, and proceeded to fabricate the costumes. We first had to decide which body parts to attempt to replicate. We decided that large organs would offer the greatest sight gags. We designed the construction first; all the pieces were to be built with technology that college students might actually have available. The first step would be to construct cardboard armatures, rough shapes taped together that would fit over the head and be the underpinnings for the shape to follow. The organ shape itself would be constructed out of sheets of soft foam, patterned, cut and glued together following the design sketches, then sprayed with latex. When the latex dried, the piece was painted and "powdered" to keep it from drying and cracking. It took ten of us almost six weeks to make everything; but when we got it all on the set it was worth it. The parade was the show-stopping scene.

The truth is, any character who stands out in some way is in a gag outfit. This might go for the clothes, a certain way of wearing the clothes, or the condition of the clothes. I always look for opportunities to use some sort of little "gag" piece, especially on bit parts, e.g., the old character hat on the cab driver who has one line in a scene with the leading actor, or the salty cardigan sweater on Grandpa.

Creating gag outfits is part of creating character. When you take the time to do it, you're creating a more interesting and authentic world for the leading actors to inhabit. It's also an area that can be a lot of fun, most especially the "treasure hunt" aspect of it. Visually, these touches separate a great film from an ordinary one.

We always look for good character and gag pieces on every pull from stock, trying to find those special items that will give the leading cast members some "honest" wardrobe to spice up their outfits with. We're always anticipating the day when, later, we will get to fit the extra crowds and the featured bit parts, as that's when we can have some fun making interesting and unusual characters whenever and wherever we wish.

A person can learn a lot about clothing, clothing manufacture, textiles, and cutting and sewing from any one of a number of fashion schools or fashion and design courses; but that's not really what motion picture costume design is about. Costume design for motion pictures is about creating mythic images, revealing character, and illustrating drama using the principles of art (especially drawing and painting, and their rules of composition, proportion, and color) and symbolism as applied to physical clothing. When clothing is used as a means of artistic expression and for dramatic insight, not as an end in itself, but as a descriptive representation in cloth for the character who wears it, it becomes a "costume." A costume designer is thus an illustrator.

On *The Last of the Mohicans* (1992 version), the designer, James Acheson, wasn't happy with the material for Daniel Day-Lewis' shirts. He had tried everything — cottons, linens, even deerskin — and didn't like any of it. He wanted something supple and lightweight, but either the texture of the materials didn't look right or they were too heavy.

We looked everywhere. I was shopping at the local Sears for tools and dye supplies, and while in the automotive section I saw packages of car-washing chamois. It was soft, supple, and strong. I bought a few packages and took them back to the shop where they were dyed a "stone" color, then gave them over to the workroom. They made a sample and James loved it. And that's the material in Daniel Day-Lewis' shirt on screen.

CHAPTER FOUR

MEETINGS: NOBODY LIKES SURPRISES

The movie business is not for people who like predictability in their life. The very nature of the business creates doubt, uncertainty, and sometimes high-stakes disagreements.

Good communication is key. Often the first production meeting on a set will determine the whole mood and tone for the entire production.

On the set of The Return of a Man Called Horse *(1976), we were shooting on location in a small town in South Dakota. At our Hollywood production meeting, we were told that our extra crowd of dressed Indians would be about fifty people, just enough to give us a little cluster around the cast. The night before shooting, the First AD told us that he had scouted the location with the director that day, and the director felt that fifty Indians just wouldn't be enough, so the extra crowd of Indians had been increased to a hundred and fifty. We had brought only about sixty-five or so outfits and didn't have the time to order any more from a costume house and have them shipped; we couldn't get any leather that fast, nor did we have anyone ready who could help us manufacture; the town was so small there wasn't even a fabric store. What to do?*

My supervisor, Bob La Bansat, was a great guy. Quite philosophical, he was always of the opinion that if all of reality is necessarily complete, when you face what you feel to be a problem you have to realize that the solution is also at hand. "After all," he told me, "a problem is only a NORMAL life circumstance for which YOU don't have a satisfactory solution. But the solution is there, no doubt." "Well, what's the solution to this?" I asked, "Where are we going to get a hundred Indian outfits by tomorrow morning?" He agreed that he didn't know. "But," he said, "if a solution seems obscure, we have to do some discovery work, and that means exploring." So exploring we went. We found a large general store, the kind only found in rural communities, looking for anything we could use... and there, hanging in one corner was a large roll of burlap. It was the right color, it was cheap, and there was a lot of it. We bought the roll, and a couple of heavy box-staplers with staples. We spent the night cutting that roll into poncho shapes, and tying strips. When the morning came, we dressed the best-looking extras in our better outfits, and then wrapped the others in outfits we had made from the burlap.

When they set the shot, they put the leather dressed extras up front and the burlap wrapped extras behind. They blended in fine. Standing there, you couldn't tell who was who. Everyone was happy. I looked at Bob, who smiled. I felt silly for worrying.

Another important department function is that you must attend meetings.

Production meetings speak for themselves. Everyone gets together in a meeting presided over by a member of Production, and everyone goes through the script page by page for red flags or production information. Most of the time, specific wardrobe questions are left for another, private meeting with the director... but, what about the rest of the crew?

On any film project there are several departments represented. All of you have to work together. So who does what and how can you prepare for them?

Politics aside, departments interact, professionally, according to each department's interests and objectives. If you can understand those, then you can better understand what will be required of your department, by whom, and when. Being able to anticipate these relationships will allow you to prepare for them and not be caught off-guard when sudden demands come at you from "out of nowhere." The good news is that on every shoot you will ever work on, the jobs will stay the same. Your only wild card will be negotiating your way through the various personalities that hold these positions, show by show.

Remember: Everyone on your show has seen someone else do your job, perhaps many times.

Costume for Sean Connery
The Wind and the Lion

ANTIQUE LACE

WHITE CHIFFON OVER
ECRU SILK

WIND & THE LION.
CANDICE BERGEN
"EDEN"
CH# 1

Costume for Candice Bergen
The Wind and the Lion

3PC TEL LINEN SUIT
IPG CUTAWAY.

ISLAND OF
DOCTOR MOREAU
BURT LANCASTER
CH # 1

Costume for Burt Lancaster
The Island of Dr. Moreau

ICLAND OF
DOCTOR MOREAU

BARBARA CARRERA

DINNER

Costume for Barbara Carrera
The Island of Dr. Moreau

GOONIES 'SLOTH' ALL CH8.

Character, "Sloth,"
Goonies

Character, "Sea Witch," *Goonies* music video
(played by Cindy Lauper's mother)

LEGEND of LIANA

Liana
Concept for TV pilot, *Legend of Liana*

1902 scout
Book illustration, "Indian scouts," John Langelier

On standard budget forms, the "talent" is separated from the "labor" by a line (for subtotaling expenditures). Therefore, everyone listed as talent is "above-the-line"; everyone listed as labor is "below-the-line." In costume design, you are below-the-line. Above-the-line personnel are producers, directors, actors, and writers. Because of their functions, above-the-line personnel are management or talent, with the ultimate power on a shoot, while other below-the-line departments are more or less your equal in terms of cooperation. Because of this, we'll go down the list as to whom you will meet, what they will (most likely) want, and how they can affect you and your job. Nobody likes surprises.

THE PRODUCER   The producer is the first person on. The project belongs to the producer, but there are different levels of producerhood.

The producer is the immediate head of production. It may be that this person had the idea originally, took it to the executive producer for funding, and is now entrusted with delivering the film for exhibition for the dollar amount raised. It may be that this person owns a production company and is delivering this project to the executive producer for exhibition, for a pre-agreed budget; either way the producer is the boss. Sometimes the producer has very definite ideas about the "look" of the project, sometimes not; sometimes the producer's interest is more dramatic or financial. Either way, you always work for the producer.

An interesting thing about this position: the producer starts the show (in construction you would call the producer the developer). A vision leads to subject matter... to a (mystical) vision of the completed project... sell this idea, and raise the money. The producer hires a writer (or is already the writer) and develops a screenplay. The idea is put into physical production. Then the producer is locked out of the process while everyone hired has the "job" of actually making the dream happen.

Producers are always entitled to have something to say about the look of productions. A lot of times they can't articulate it except in the general sense of wanting it to be "good" or "realistic"; sometimes they are very sophisticated about technical matters, including sets, costumes, and props.

A concept meeting, early on, with the producer, is important. Find out what the producer wants. The question is, "How demanding does the producer want to be?" Sometimes producers leave you alone. Sometimes they're people you have to convince. They may demand that you do something you hate; they may know more than you do... you have to find out. Be relaxed and courteous, it's their show and you're always there to help them.

EXECUTIVE PRODUCER You may never meet this person. The executive producer gets the money to fund the movie. Sometimes this person will never show up, the job being more a function of money than the day-to-day process of shooting. My experience is that they leave the creative decisions up to others.

LINE PRODUCER This person has the direct responsibility of making the film, day-to-day, within predetermined budget guidelines. In construction, this would be the general contractor. Line Producers hire the workforce. Many technicians aim their responsibility at this position. This person works show to show and often re-hires the same people — people who are financially responsible and, at the same time, please the producer and director with their results. Usually not dictatorial about the film's look, line producers are always budget-centered. They hate spending money unnecessarily, and will be very interested in your budget and your ideas about running your department. This is the person to whom you will have to justify your numbers. These folks are usually industry savvy, have a lot of budget experience, and have seen your job done before by someone else. A sound, well-prepared department plan will go a long way with this person. When convinced of your position, this person will be the one to get you what you need. Line producers NEVER LIKE SURPRISES! Stay with them weekly on expenditures and money projections.

DIRECTOR Most people know what this job is. Originally a job more technical than creative, the director was charged with getting performances out of the actors, while the staging was left to the cinematographer. The director worked more with the editor in shooting the required angles for splicing together later to form the story-telling, while the design was left to the art director (sets) and costume designer (including hair and makeup).

All this has changed with the auteur theory of filmmaking: Nowadays the director is the FINAL AUTHORITY on the set and decides almost everything about what goes in front of the camera. Thus the director is the person who will feel in direct control. The director has been hired by the producer to use moviemaking skill and taste to put the story on film. Everything needs the director's stamp of approval. For this reason, concept meetings with the director are a must! The director will be keenly interested in the costume illustration. A director's job is to combine all the elements: photography, lighting, sets, costumes, effects, editing, and actors' performances into a credible, visual, dramatic interpretation. In a sense directors are also the directors of design, so you have to work closely with them to come to a shared vision that you can pour yourself into; use research, show-and-tells, costume parades, concept sketches... whatever it takes.

A word about the director's authority. Directors have all the authority that the producers agree to let them have, according to the deal and the budget. There can be a problem here that you will meet on production, and it's called, "Whose show is it anyway?"

There are times when the line producer and the director are not sharing the same vision.

Here's an example. The director tells you to get overcoats for everybody. You hire the overcoats... telling the line producer... who says, "Tell the director, 'No! They're not in the budget.'" What do you do? I would advise this: If anybody, director and producer included, asks you for anything in addition to your agreed budget, be calm, positive, and optimistic; then get a dollar amount and talk to the line producer. On some films, the money is there. The director may *be* the producer, and the answer will be, "What are you waiting for?" But this won't always be the case. Sometimes the answer will be a very definite "NO!" Find out before you spend money. If there is a production department disagreement about what should or shouldn't be spent, get them to talk to each other — get out of the middle.

ACTORS   There are as many situations as there are actors and movies, some are insecure demanding prim donnas; some are laid back and easy;

some are tasteless or surrounded by entourages full of political intrigue; some are highly intelligent and very tasteful. Again, most have seen your job done by someone else, perhaps many times.

Best-case scenario: you love and admire each other and each other's work. You create together in an atmosphere of support and trust to develop a mutual artistic vision whose dazzling brightness sparkles in the imagination of all.

Worst-case scenario: An actor bitches and moans, complains, ridicules, demeans and embarrasses you, finally arguing hysterically over some nonsensical, never-discussed trivial item, and gets you fired.

In other words, it's all ego... but what do you expect? Actors are people who have to display their fears, insecurities, and vulnerabilities to large and indifferent audiences for a living. Most of the time they will respond to you if your design plan is sound because they know that they will be cared for, and that they are receiving the benefit of YOUR expertise in assembling the costume tools from which they will fashion their character. Some are more collaborative than others. In general, the higher on the cast sheet, the more actors are allowed to demand. Then again, the higher on the cast sheet, the more secure good actors are, and can be the *least* demanding. Be prepared. Be secure in yourself. Have a plan. Be gracious and flexible.

Modern shows are, sometimes, harder than period shows. The reason is simple: On period shows, most people will defer to the costume designer as long as everything looks right. On modern shows, everyone's the expert. Everyone has opinions, and some are thinking about what they will be wearing home AFTER the show. So it all takes finesse.

Years ago at Fox, they told me: "Never be friends with actors." The idea is always to be friendly, but never friends. The reason is that actors have full lives too. They might desire camaraderie on the set, but they are not there to be your buddy. Professionalism dictates that you always be gracious with them but keep a respectful, professional, personal, and social distance that allows them the freedom to withdraw mentally when they have to prepare. You never, never bug them with personal issues on the set. I have found this to be very good advice. You're a professional designer, not a groupie, and not a valet.

FIRST ASSISTANT DIRECTOR   Known as the First AD. If the director directs the cast, then the First AD directs the crew. The set belongs to First ADs. They are directly responsible to the line producer to get the crew organized and keep the director on schedule. Their problems are many. They do not like surprises or excuses. They run the AD Department, which is, officially, like the eyes and ears of Production. They belong to the same Directors Guild as the director and unit production manager or line producer... and they talk together about everything on the show.

First ADs also have a hand in scheduling and coming up with the extra day count. You'll want to jump on the First AD as *soon* as possible, to get a fix on how many extras you will enjoy in any one set, and the latest thoughts on the schedule. Both these pieces of information are CRUCIAL to your department. How many costumes do you need, what works first and where? The impact on your work schedule is dynamic. Everything you do, department-wise, apart from the creative, will be to facilitate the First AD's set operation and schedule. Constantly ask questions. Be persistent in getting show schedule information, and match your department needs against it. Build a relationship that will be lasting and cooperative. First ADs are your biggest source for "inside information," for production changes, and for new show information. The key set costumer will work closely with the First AD as set changes occur through the day. One of the keys to running a department on location is ANTICIPATION, the ability to see what's coming. And whatever it is, it will most likely come from the First AD.

PRODUCTION DESIGNER   This title is relatively recent. Production designers used to be called art directors, and their job was to design and oversee the construction of the sets and their decoration. Some time in the seventies the job of production designer came about because it was felt that one person was needed to sit with the director from day one to conceive ("concept") the show. So everything that goes in front of the camera is thought of now as part of a cohesive design concept that falls under the responsibility of the production designer.

This is a relationship where you will need to tread lightly. Most production designers are not costume trained, and don't want to take over your department... but in the initial phases they will want to, and have the right to, comment on the direction of your design concept. They are BIG on color. Everything you know about color theory, color percentage and value, will be a help. They tend to put a lot of stock into old paintings as research. With regard to color usage, see Rembrandt, Norman Rockwell, Frederick Remington, Winslow Homer, N. C. Wyeth, and John Singer Sargent for openers.

Professional courtesy is the key. Remember, production designers are usually already working on the show by the time you show up; they have heard more from the director about the "look" than you have at this point. These are, usually, seasoned professional artists. Once they find they like what you're doing, they'll let you do your thing... so listen, learn, be happy.

PROPERTY DEPARTMENT   My favorite. If costumers are "rag pickers," then prop people are "junkers." The best on-set working relationship you can have will be with the prop person. All the stuff on the set, everything the decorator left behind to dress, belongs to the prop person. Everything your actor removes or puts on during the course of a scene belongs to the prop person. All jewelry, watches, bags, swords, guns, etc. are props. If you read in the script that a particular piece of wardrobe has "action," that means it's an "action prop" (i.e., it has a described action in the script) so it belongs to the prop person.

Wardrobe and Property have to help each other build the show together. This relationship started in theater, on the stage, and has been around for hundreds of years. Actors walked and talked the action, while backstage responsibilities were divided according to "set-scene-scenic." "Scenic," that is, the background, included set design (art directors), construction (sets), painters (backdrops), plaster (staff shops), and grips (rigging). "Set," that is, the foreground, meant set design (plans), decorators (dressing), and grips (moving set pieces as stagehands). "Scene," that is, the foreground which included the actors and director, also involved the costumes and hand props. The actors just wore what they wore; sometimes they brought it with them in a large trunk. Used to playing the same parts in play after play, they accumulated their own costumes. When actors got to the theater they turned their trunks over to the prop person. The prop person gave the costumes to the laundry person to freshen and repair while they accessorized the characters with swords, jewelry, skulls, scrolls, breakaway bottles, etc.

Today the Wardrobe/Property relationship hasn't changed much as far as "how to think of the stuff" is concerned. On shows like Westerns or action movies, where a lot of belt equipment, helmets, and the like is worn, the question always arises, "Who will carry this or that and whose budget will pay for it?" The old rule of thumb was, if it goes in a dressing room for an actor, who goes to makeup with it, it's Costumes. If it's issued off a truck AFTER the actor is dressed, it's Prop. If it's handed to the actor and taken from the actor on the set, it's a prop.

No matter what, there WILL be crossover pieces between Costumes and Property... so work it out early. The property department can be your biggest asset on the set if you have a good working relationship. These can be clever, artistic, and very knowledgeable people. Work together, they are interested in the same things you are as far as the actor and their characters are concerned.

CAMERA DEPARTMENT   They call this business "motion pictures" — not "motion sound" or "motion costumes." The director of photography, or "DP" is the head recordist. This is another relationship that you have to feel out... but generally, they are there to photograph the movie, not dictate what it looks like. Your mutual area of concern will be color, especially whites and off-whites.

Working on *The Wind and the Lion*, I designed, and had built a beautiful period dress. It was a symphony of cream chiffon over a body of tan silk. The actress wore it to the set on a Saturday, to show the director, as we were shooting it Monday. The director loved it. The DP looked long... mused... and said, "Well, I can't shoot it." Time stopped. "It's too bright," he said, "too white. You'll have to do something about it." Back in the department I huddled over the dress with the wardrobe crew. We had used up all our tan dye, and tomorrow, Sunday, everything was closed. "Bleach," said the laundry person. "Dye it grey, then bleach it, and it will come tan." We heated the water in a fifty-five gallon drum... poured in packets of grey dye... dunked the dress. It went from an angelic vision to a drowned rat. We lifted the dress, gently wrung it out. We could see the chiffon shrinking. We all grabbed corners and pulled away from each other while one person steamed with an iron. It sort of worked. The dress went on, was photographed and was okay, skimpy but wearable, definitely not the flowing, romantic piece we all had in mind. The moral: Always check with the DP.

DECORATION DEPARTMENT   These folks will ask you for clothes to dress the sets: suitcases, drawers, clotheslines. My answer is always, "I can only afford enough clothes to dress the people I have to. If you need clothes for dressing, please give me a list and I'll rent them for you on your department budget, or you can select them yourself. After the show, YOU will be responsible for returning them to the rental house, thank you." There are times when they want to use a piece of principal wardrobe because it will tie a character in... and that's okay, I'll give it to them before the shot and take it back after the shot. But in general, costumes are costumes and dressing is dressing. If they lose or destroy something they borrow, you will pay for it. Plus, you will lose the use of the clothes while they have them, may be longer than you think. Have them get their own.

STUNT DEPARTMENT   Another one of my favorites. I've had a lot of friends in this department over the years. As a set person I was detailed, many times, to "take care" of them and their costume needs. They are, by definition, hard on clothes.

I always make it a point to make contact with the stunt coordinator as soon as I can to find out the sizes of his or her stunt crew; who will be doubling the cast and their sizes; and what, if any, safety rigging or equipment will be necessary, including fireproofing or flying rig harnesses. If it's an action piece, will the clothes that look tight on the actor have to be gusseted for the stunt double who will perform the action? Will the leather sole shoes have to be covered with rubber for nonslip traction? If I don't get answers on sizes, I take oversized clothes for them to wear over stunt pads.

On Westerns or war films, the amount of multiples used for bullet hits, progressive aging and plain destruction from hard use can be hard on your department budget if you're not prepared for it. Also, the stunt coordinator might also be the second unit director. Now's the time to find out how ambitious that second unit will be, and whether you'll need a lot of extra clothes and have to hire help to service it.

TRANSPORTATION DEPARTMENT Trucks, trailers, and sometimes tents on location are "Transpo" items. I've always found that these people do what they can to help facilitate your needs. Give them as much advanced warning as possible about the movement and location spotting of your equipment.

ACCOUNTING DEPARTMENT The two functions of accounting are: time card/payroll; and POs (purchase orders), petty cash, and vendor payments. Time card/payroll speaks for itself. Accounting makes sure we all get paid. As far as POs go, the system for purchases is usually cumbersome and not geared for speed. Some of your immediate purchase problems can be more easily solved with a petty cash draw. When it comes to vendors, I always walk my vendor bills through Accounting to be sure that they are paid promptly. I tend to use a lot of the same vendors over and over. I have business-friendly relationships with them. If I need something right away, I know I can call several sources and they will send me the things I need, immediately, ON MY WORD. They do this because they know that I will take care of their bill as soon as it comes in, period. Your ability to pull rabbits out of hats is only as good as your sources.

I also get used to checking with the show accountant on the status of my department expenditures on a weekly basis, in order to keep track of where I am in relation to my budget.

MAKEUP-AND-HAIR DEPARTMENT As a designer, the biggest interface will concern facial hair, hair styles and the wearing of hats or hair ornaments. This includes anything a Native American (or anyone else) might wear in their hair, or material for braid-ties. Women's hats are set in and pinned in the hair trailer as well, meaning that hats have to be taken there and collected every day. Hair style research, especially for the cast, should be shared between the designer, makeup and hair supervisor, and director to agree on the look. Things tend to get lost in doing crowds. Do you need braid wraps, feathers, or custom-made ornaments? Get more than you think you'll need.

CASTING DEPARTMENT   Here's where the actors come from... and this is information you want as soon as possible. Remind the director that as soon as actors are signed, you need to be informed right away.

EFFECTS DEPARTMENT   Again, these people are hard on clothes. Find out early what their requirements are for multiples of costumes. If there will be large battle scenes, you might want to park your department close to the effects truck, because those will be days when you'll have to work together.

WRANGLERS   Mostly these people work on Westerns. They will always drive the wagons and sometimes ride horses in the shot. They are the hardest people to keep track of because they work (both before and after shooting) with the livestock. I love them, but they get used to throwing the clothes in the back of the horse trailer, then bringing them back in a dirty pile.

PRODUCTION COORDINATOR   This person can save your life on location. A good production coordinator will get shipments in and out for you when you need something but you're locked on the set. Production coordinators know when the actors arrive and where they are staying. They can and will try to set up fittings for you, including getting actors transported to the set and back.

TECHNICAL ADVISOR   Some TAs are a bigger influence than others on the director. I always make it a point to bring in the technical advisor as early as I can to go over everything. If the technical advisor has a problem with anything that affects my budget, I get a meeting with the line producer and find out what the company wants me to do. For instance, do I rent the uniform that isn't quite right but close, or do I spend ten times the amount to build the "correct" one that the TA wants? Some TAs are much more understanding and helpful than others. Find out who's on your show and work accordingly; but always remind the TA of the cost whenever suggestions are made.

Recently I finished a military pilot about Vietnam. One night on location, six new actors came in to work for the next day. The director wanted all of them in fitted uniforms. I was in the tailor shop pinning outfits for alterations when a call came in on the set walkie-talkie: the technical advisor had told the director that Wardrobe was sewing patches on wrong. The director was very upset with us and wanted to see research right away. I was right in the middle of fittings and couldn't leave the actors and seamstress for the hour it would take to unpack the research and take the drive up the trail to the set and back, so I told the set person that we were right, but just go ahead and do whatever the technical advisor said and I would square it later. When I got to the set with the research, I found that thankfully the company medic, a Vietnam vet, had beat me to it with his own in-country photographs to prove us right. But even so the technical advisor had planted that seed of doubt with the director that never quite died out. That lack of trust haunted us to the end. Sometimes even being right isn't enough.

GRIP DEPARTMENT   These people handle the set carpentry and lighting. I always start a show by telling the key grip that I have access to a sewing machine and will be happy to make sandbags, repair their silks, add "floppies" to the flags, etc. This gesture endears you to the grips right away. When working the set I always help them move apple boxes or whatever. Grips carry century (or "C") stands to hold their diffusion and/or flags. These "C" stands can be used for temporary cloth racks on location behind camera. Grips are usually happy to let you use them; be sure to return the stands when you're finished or next time they might "not have enough."

ELECTRIC DEPARTMENT   These folks might hook up your work lights, lend you extension cords, or help your department with some electrical problem. Always be kind.

SOUND DEPARTMENT   This is a department that will work with the set costumer all the time regarding the placement of microphones, wires, and transmitters. I check with the sound technicians to see if they need small pouches with waist ties to secure their transmitters around the waists of the actors; if they don't have them, I make them. (If Sound doesn't have these pouches, they may just cut holes inside your pants or coat pockets to string the wire from the microphone to the transmitter in the actor's pocket.)

Every expendable store carries "sound booties." These are black or white slip-ons, overshoes made of flannel; they're designed to muffle footfalls on wood floors. Ask Sound if these are needed.

One more thing: The sound department hates silk. Sensitive sound equipment hears the rustle of a silk tie or blouse when a microphone is a small clip-on type. The only solution is to change the garment or change the mike.

CHAPTER 5

ACCUMULATING THE COSTUMES

Rambo III *(1988) presented an interesting challenge for Costume Design. The movie was about the Russian invasion of Afghanistan, which at that time, you could see broadcast on the six-o'clock news. I realized that the costumes for this film had to look as real and authentic as possible. The clothing just didn't exist for rent at any costume house, American or English. The supervisor, Darrel Athons, located an Afghan importer, Sadiq Towfig, who suggested that we go to the Khyber pass area of Pakistan where the Afghan refugee camps were located and purchase all the costume and props that we needed. We discussed it with the producer, Buzz Feitchens, who agreed that it made sense and the trip was on. We spent a couple of weeks hanging out with the Mujahadeen, who were wintering in their camps, buying clothing, jewelry, props and dressing. We had some memorable times sitting on carpeted floors, and eating with our fingers while listening to their warrior stories by lantern light.*

The film itself was shot in Israel. There's a place so packed with history that you can't go a hundred yards without someone pointing out things like: "See that valley, that's where David fought Goliath," "See that village, that's where Sampson was born." We would get the tour buses on weekends and visit the famous Biblical sites. While we were there, there was a three-day weekend. The company was shut down, so a few of us hopped a flight to Cairo, stayed at the Ramses Hilton on the Nile, climbed around the pyramids, took the dinner barge up the Nile, then drove back on the old caravan road.

When the location in Israel was finished, we shot the opening of the film in Thailand. That was another adventure. From the modern and exotic city of Bangkok to the rainy mountain area around Chiang Mai, I spent a month, shopping, preparing the department, and shooting.

> *Postscript: Sadiq, the Afghan importer, and I are planning to go into business this year, importing textiles and furnishings including oriental rugs... looks like more travel for me.*

In order to find the costumes you need, you have to develop an angle of attack.

What I mean by this is that you have to have a plan; and that plan has to be specific to your show and department requirements. How and where are you going to get the things that you need? Part of the problem has been solved by a couple of things you've already done. Your costume breakdown and budget package have in it the amounts and types of costumes, researched, that you'll be seeking. To get quotes, you will have had to talk to rental houses for information on the availability of the clothing that you require.

SMALL PROJECTS   These are projects that require fewer than a hundred outfits. Many people are involved with commercials, print ad, or small film projects in a regional area that isn't convenient to major costume rental houses. If this is your situation, then you know to depend more on yourself and a network you've built up of vendors and local craftspeople to fill your needs. These sources might include a local theater or college drama department (for hanging stock and/or personnel), local specialty manufacture artisans, leather shops, jewelry makers, metal workers, and the like.

If you get a requirement for things that exceed your local resources, and if you're not nearby a major costume rental house, you can still call them to inquire if they have the stock you need; if they sound helpful and knowledgeable, talk overall concept as well as specifics. They might have some good ideas, based on the stock they know they have. (See the Appendix for a list of costume houses.)

Expect to pay fifty dollars or so to have them send you Polaroids of examples of the stock you're seeking. Be prepared to fax them simple line drawings of what you want (photos and/or Xeroxes don't fax well). Discuss prices, both "weekly" (short-term) and "production" (long-term), as they will differ from house to house.

If it's a phone order to a costume house in another state, have all your business information ready: name, business name, fax and phone number, billing address, shipping address, credit card number with name and address of card holder, FedEx account number, date you need the costumes, date you will ship the costumes back, and a concise list of the costumes you need, with their colors and sizes. Speaking of sizes, women's dress sizes are usually not very reliable; the sizes change with period, pattern, maker, and label, so a size eight from the forties could be a four today. Always get a bust, waist, hip, height, neck, sleeve, and (depending on the length of the garment) a waist-to-knee, waist-to-floor, or waist-to-hem measurement.

Men's clothes are usually sized with measurements anyway, but with men always give the pant inseam length, as the outseam length will vary from period to period with the cut (high-rise or low-rise). Remember, with thirties and forties pants, the rise is so high that men can wear a shorter inseam because of the drop in the crotch.

If you have a little lead time, ask the costume house if you can establish credit. It's easy to get the costume house accountant to send you a credit application, which you can then have the company you're working for fill out and return for you. This way, you can place orders and the company will be billed with no charges to the credit card (which you might want to save for other things). If you have to use a credit card, expect a "reserve" hold on the card against loss and damage equal to two to three times the rental amount.

RENTAL HOUSES AND THE PACKAGE DEAL Larger projects, where you will get the clothes and need to make a money deal favorable to you, will take some analyzing. Let's look at the internal workings of a costume house first. A costume house is first and foremost a business. In order to stay in business it has to meet its obligated expenses. It has to make money by renting, selling, or making costumes to fill show requirements for designers and supervisors and ultimately for producers and studios.

A little history: Western Costume is the oldest running costume business in the country. It goes back to the turn of the last century when it started as an "Indian trading post" that provided Native American costumes for silent Westerns. During the thirties and forties, all the major studio lots owned a piece of "Western" and ran it, communally, as a storage facility. If the rental facility went in the red at the end of the year, then the Studios pitched in to cover expenses.

In the fifties, costume rental facilities started to be run as independent businesses that had to meet overhead expenditures; they did this by charging rent on costumes and paying attention to the bottom line.... Prices rose.

During the seventies, with the rise of independent films and the shrinking of lot departments, studio employees who had an entrepreneurial spirit started to rent space and created "off-the-lot" departments. This actually happened across the board, with Props, Grips, Electric, Camera, Makeup, Transportation, Catering, Postproduction, Script Services, and more. Every department that had been up until then "on the lot" now sprung up off-the-lot to compete financially. And so it remains today.

Each independent costume rental facility is different — with a unique corporate personality, staff, physical space, and hanging stock. They are similar in the purchasing and manufacture resources available to them, and identical in their mission, which is of course to get costumers what they want, charge them enough money to stay in business, and, God willing, make a profit.

There are two ways to look at any business relationship. When dealing with people, you either view it as a partnership or as an adversarial standoff.

Often, people hired on a show will put themselves in an adversarial position with the very people who are there to help them. Let's look at where you are and what you're trying to do at this point: You have been hired and have made a commitment to deliver a show's requirements. You have a certain amount of money to work with (never enough), and a finite number of hours to round up all your requirements and to be where you're supposed to be when it's time to start shooting. Your objectives are threefold:

1. Get everything you can.

2. Get it all as fast as you can.

3. Get it as cheap as you can.

Now let's look at the mission of the costume house:

1. Give you what they can.

2. Get it all as fast as they can.

3. Charge you as much as they can.

Adversarial businesspeople favor competitive shopping. It goes like this... "How much do you charge for a shirt?... How much do you charge for a dress?" You do this with your list of requirements, times the amount of costume houses you can find. You learn that all the prices are about the same; you might hear that this one will give you a discount or that one will beat "anyone's price." You then try to figure out where you can stretch your rental budget further as you are also trying to figure out how much you should keep back for manufacture and purchases... it feels like it's you against the world.

If you start pulling from every house in town, you'll find that no one has much time to help you. You might explain that you are trying to spread your money around because you owe a favor, or because you want to "help everyone a little"; but if you ask for a discount you'll probably be refused because "your order is too small." In this case, you'll also feel disgruntled when you're told that you can't rent partial outfits, or they say "we don't accessorize."

Think WalMart. How do they give such low prices? Volume. The power to lower rental prices is "amortization." In other words, from a costume house point of view, the more you take, including purchases and manufacture, the more they can lower the price. Let's say that your budget is fifty thousand dollars... but you are quoted fifty thousand in rentals plus ten thousand in purchases... you can't afford it... you plead with the costume house to give you fifty thousand dollars' worth of rentals for forty thousand so you can afford the ten for purchases... they say maybe they'll give you ten percent, that's it. What can you do? You keep shopping around while your time runs out.

From the costume house side, if I were the manager, I would look at it this way. You want a certain amount of clothing. I have company-set prices. I have to think about how much of MY labor I will have to spend to get my side of your show ready. I may have to spend a certain amount to complete the outfits that you've ordered. I already know I have a price sheet that's fair and competitively priced. I know that you're getting things from other places. In some cases you're not even getting complete outfits from me, you've found cheaper prices somewhere else, but you like some of my stuff better... so you want to get the suits from Joe down the block, but you want to rent the hats and shoes from me. Well, my answer would be "No." Why? Number one, you aren't being a good customer... sorry, that's the answer. Two, no way am I going to accessorize your show with hats and shoes. Why not? If I let you take my hats and shoes, and the next costumer that comes to me wants to rent complete outfits, I won't be able to, because you have the hats and shoes. If you've broken everything up into small units based on competitive pricing or individual service prices, I have to stick to my prices, because everything I give you will have to "pay for itself."

This strategy will result in more pressure on you and not much savings. This is a no-win situation for everyone. It's adversarial.

What's the answer? Partnership.

Let's look again at the same situation. I'm the costume house manager, and you tell me up front that you only have fifty thousand dollars, but you need fifty thousand dollars' worth of rentals and ten thousand dollars' worth of purchases. Instead of sitting across the table, we can take chairs on the same side. We find out how we can do this together based on the amount YOU have to spend. The key is to be frank, open, and honest; your financial situation or requirements won't change, but the attitude of the costume house will.

As the manager I have to assess whether I want your purchases. If I do, then I just might make that deal — give you everything, rentals and purchases, for the fifty you have to spend. Why? Easy, I'm using the rental profits to absorb the purchases (provided I get them back), where I will be able to count them as equity for my FUTURE rental profit.

That combining of budget requirements, rentals, purchases, and manufacture into a lump-sum bottom-line figure is called a *package deal*, and it always works the same way. It uses the power of the money spent in rentals to absorb the cost of purchases and/or manufacture. If you are talking only about lowering the price of the rentals, you can still call it a package, but it's really just a discounted rental price.

The financial ability of any costume house to lower prices by combining elements in your budget will always be based on the rental volume you do with them, because the more business you give them, on off-the-rack stock items, the larger rental income base it gives them for spreading other costs, i.e., amortization.

Always look at the hanging stock in a rental house with this in mind. Find the house that has THE MOST stock that can go toward your show and construct your package deal there — everything at one place. If you want a few things from other places, talk about it ahead of time, and reserve some of your budget money for "outside rentals." Find out how much they will throw in if you do the bulk of the show there, e.g., office, cage, discount on a trailer. Most places know that they are competing for the same dollars on your show, so when they see that you're serious, they get serious.

You can use your cast and background breakdown sheets to give them an idea of what's required of them. Figure out and tell them how much of your show you can do from their stock plus how much you expect them to make or buy. Then they can figure out whether or not they can afford to work with you within your budget.

Another important point to consider. When you are on a distant location, you have an emergency and you have to call back to town for help... whom do you want on the other end of the line? Who has the best reserve of stuff, and who is the most dependable? This is the costume house to choose.

Some things are harder to get than others. If you're getting things from several places, some people will feel that you're giving them the "hard" stuff while you're giving someone else the "gravy." Remember, you might cross the desert with a hundred different caravans but you will always drink at the same few wells. If you plan to have anything made at a costume house with costume house labor, discuss everything. Sometimes costumers are not clear on who owns what at the end of the show, or they are put off by a twenty-five or thirty-five percent addition to a manufacture price for loss and damage, especially after they paid to have it made. The house answer is: "We made it for you at our cost. If you don't return it, we have to add on our profit margin, or basically we did it for nothing." That always confused me until I really thought about it.

Sometimes, the deal will be easy; just a straightforward rental. No matter what the size or shape of the deal is, you will need to arrange to pay them something, sometime.

Of course, when striking any deal, be sure to address the loss and damage prices. Find out in advance what the house plans to charge you in both general and specific prices. If they give you a "good" deal going in, then you might expect "full book" (full price) replacement on the way out. See if they will accept exchanges for losses (your own location purchases or outside manufacture items, for example).

You will also have to determine a "benchmark draw-down schedule," which decides upon the dates your company will make payments to the house. Sometimes it's a third down, another third half-way through prep, and the last third before the costumes leave the house. Sometimes, it's half down and half before the costumes leave. Sometimes you will have until the end of the show to finish paying, or it can be something else, but you have to work this out ahead of time, along with the size of the deposit for loss and damage and final show cleaning, which is a separate cost.

On shows where the costume house and the producer are at odds over the price or payment schedule, you can find yourself in the middle of THEIR negotiation, being asked to carry figures back and forth. If this happens, I would advise you to get THEM together to work things out. Stand back until THEY are both satisfied that the deal that they agree to is the best deal they can make. Being in the middle puts you in an awkward position with everyone; but show politics may dictate that you get in there and try your hand at negotiating. The company, your employer, will, of course expect that you get the best price for them that you can. If you are dedicated to your budget, you will want to get the best deal that you can for yourself. In this sense you are acting as an agent for your employer, which means you have the legal fiduciary duty to act in their best interest.

However, as a professional costume person you will also have understanding for the problems of the rental house. You will, in a professional sense, want the costume house to make money in order to stay in business so that they will continue to be a resource for you in the future.

Somewhere within those interests lies the deal that everyone can live with. It takes a special attitude to negotiate successfully. You have to see and be sympathetic to all sides, be both passionate and detached, work in your own best interests. See where the other fellow can give, and point it out while keeping in good spirits. Arguing will only make people dig in and become more intractable. You want a deal that everyone thinks is fair while you are satisfied that it's a little more fair to you. When you realize that a costume budget can run into the thousands, or hundreds of thousands of dollars, you can easily imagine that you are sitting at the table in a large-stakes card game. In fact, that's how a lot of people look at it. The process has raises, bluffs, and all. For further insight, you might want to read books on negotiating; there are some good ones out there, available at any bookstore.

Accumulating costumes can often be a mechanical process, but sometimes the need to find original and interesting costumes creates new opportunities and adventures that make me appreciate the uniqueness of this business.

When I was growing up I always wanted to travel, but never thought I'd have the opportunity. As it worked out I've gotten to travel more than I ever dreamed I would or could. While I've had the opportunity to see many interesting places on film locations, two films stand out as having offered real adventures. Years ago on *The Wind and the Lion*, I spent about four months in Spain. We traveled from the mountains of the north to the sandy beaches of the south, visiting ancient Moorish castles and gardens as shooting locations. As if that weren't enough, I took a shopping trip to Morocco and spent a couple of weeks touring the country — from Tangiers through the Atlas mountains — visiting Berber villages and the ancient Arab cities of Fez, Tetouan, and others just looking for costumes and jewelry for cast and background. When the film finished shooting I had saved enough money out of my per diem to buy a couple of Eurail passes and even to fly my wife over. We flew to Rome and started a two-week hippie train tour that took us to Venice, Florence, Vienna, Munich, Bern, Paris, Amsterdam, and London. This is a trip we'll never forget.

PULLING YOUR SHOW   They used to tell us at Fox, "Look at everything two ways, what it is and what it can be." So if you can't find what you want, what's close to it?

Remember, the object is to get everything you can use as fast as you can. The reasons are these: First, you want to see what you have to work with so that you can find any problem areas that will require time to address. Second, you want to look for anything that might be "cast" material, for wear or samples. You also want to get everything you can, that you like, before someone else, pulling a similar show, gets it.

Your background breakdown pages are your guide. You can break them up among your labor force and have everyone (or you alone) look for and complete a costume pull one page at a time, one group at a time. The way things are hung in most costume houses is by alike groups, so if you're pulling a page of police, for example, most of it will be together. You can complete each group, check the colors and sizes, check for completeness (are additional costume house purchases required to fill holes?), see if repairs are needed, etc. Get each group checked off, start the billing and move on to the next group.

Just a couple of guidelines to keep in mind while pulling. Always check the garment for needed repairs. Always check the inside waistband of men's pants for alterations; if they have been taken in a lot, then the leg will be too wide proportionally. Check pant cuffs and dress hems for any "let-down," and if they don't have any, be sure they meet your minimum length requirement.

If I'm working on a tight budget and can only rent enough outfits to fill my extra count with little or no "fitting allowance," I line up my group of outfits by size, starting with the smallest, and make sure that if I'm taking five small hats, then I'm also taking five small shirts, coats, vests, pants, and shoes. That is, you don't want to be issuing clothes to extras and then half-way through discover that you pulled everything you liked because of the color and texture, but now you have only small coats, large vests, and medium pants left.

The best way to do it is to put up your sizes on a curve — five to ten percent small, fifteen to twenty percent medium, fifty to sixty percent large (with ten percent of those longs), ten to fifteen percent extra-large, and five percent double-extra-large. Be sure to check with casting about the area of your location and the average size of the people there.

PURCHASES If you're looking for unusual things, things not sold in stores at the mall... look in the magazine stand first. There are a lot of areas of special interest, which have a large enough following to have their own magazines. Everything from sports to militaria to antiques have their own magazines devoted to their particular subjects. Usually, the backs of those magazines are full of special-interest ads from vendors who specialize in making and selling things to people who share that particular interest. Perusing these magazines and a diligent phone pursuit, based on business-to-business directories, will usually pay off. And now, of course, we have the world at our fingertips via the Internet.

The other way to accumulate clothing is to manufacture it yourself. There are only three ways to think of M.O (made-to-order). Either you make the costumes under your direct supervision with your own labor; you contract them out to someone else to make; or you have things made at a costume house. We've already looked at all three in Chapter 3 Costume Design, but since we're here, there might be a few other things I could add.

The reasons to take on any manufacture are simple: You can't find what you want hanging for rent. Or you expect a lot of loss and damage and don't want to pay twice.

If you choose to contract them out, be sure to HAVE a contract. Be sure to include everything: who pays for materials, overtime, and shipping;

and the dates when samples are to be approved, clothes finished, and the all-important delivery date!

Dealing with a vendor for the first time? You will want to pad the final delivery date in order to insure that if the vendor is a little late it still won't hurt.

Most vendors will want fifty percent down and fifty percent on delivery. Expect that and budget accordingly.

SPECIALTY MANUFACTURE This includes: silk screen, Vacu-form, latex, metalwork, castings, embroidery, all the non-sewing-machine manufacture that might help you build your costumes. These craftspeople usually advertise in the yellow pages. Printing your own material, or making your own armor or other special skill work will mean that, unless you have access to the talent directly, you will be hiring from these businesses. If you're seeking local, non-union costume labor, you might also look for help from costume shops, college theater departments, civic operas, or neighborhood theaters. Union shows done on the west coast are staffed by the Costumers Local #705. A call to their business office will get you all the information you will need to find and hire well-qualified union members as costumers or tailors. There are several pages of business and personal ads in *LA 411* or in the *Hollywood Creative Directory* series (available at larger Southern California newsstands or bookstores).

CHAPTER SIX

AGING AND DISTRESSING

The Island of Dr. Moreau *(1977) was about a mad doctor (Burt Lancaster) who was trying to make humans out of animals. The experiments weren't working and his island home was filled with creatures, half-human, half-man. The makeup created by Stan Chambers was extensive but no one wanted to see the creatures nude, so the question arose, "What would the creatures wear?" It was thought that they might wear cast-off clothing from Moreau, but the idea of all these "hum-animals" running around in regular clothing seemed silly... What to do?*

I lined up a lot of really distressed character clothing. While a lot of it looked great, and indeed, some of the creatures would wear "real" clothing; everything was just too recognizable. I had to find some way to obscure it. I finally got an idea. I took cheesecloth, dyed it a mouse-gray color, then shot the garments with spray glue and stuck on the cheesecloth in layers, letting a lot of it hang in shreds. It did the trick: the cheesecloth muted the color while imparting a texture that was uniform and unrecognizable.

As we've already mentioned briefly, aging is done to give a costume character. It means taking a new piece and making it look old and worn.

There are a lot of ways to age clothing, but no matter how much you do, you will always be using the same supplies, so let's go over the most important ones.

FULLERS EARTH

This is a very fine sifted powder that can be purchased at any costume rental house (and some paint stores). Fullers Earth is the generic name for all colored sifted earth, but it also refers to a specific dark taupe color. There is also ROTTENSTONE, which is lighter, and looks like concrete powder. BURNT UMBER is very dark brown; RAW UMBER has a red cast to it. LAMP BLACK is pure black. You can also find these powders in RED OXIDE and RAW SIENNA or BURNT SIENNA. Be careful. These powders are very fine, and because of that, they get into everything if not used with caution. NEVER use them in a room where things have to be kept clean, or on a table that will be used for a cutting table. If used with the right vehicle these powders are a good dry pigment for mixing paint.

A "grease rag" is used all the time and you can make one with the same powders. You can apply them with various mediums — water, Lexol, mineral oil, even gesso, gel, alcohol, in other words, just about anything. Lexol and mineral oil are favored because of the easy spread and speed of application. A piece of terry cloth is soaked with oil, then filled with the "Earth" and smashed around until the surface of the rag is completely covered by the dark paste combination. The rag is then rolled and kept in a plastic zip bag until needed. The rag can be wiped around cuffs, collars, elbows, knees, anywhere you want dirt to show. For subtler touchups, use your fingers after wiping them on the grease rag.

HAIR SPRAY

Comes in various colors. Can be diluted with water into streaks or modeled with a damp rag or sponge.

LEATHER SPRAY

Comes in a great variety of colors. Used for changing the color of leather.

HOUSE PAINT

Either spray or in a liquid can, house paint has many and varied uses. Can create a wide variety of finishes and textures.

SPRITZ BOTTLES

Hudson sprayers and Flachettes are for spraying a controlled amount of water on your work surface.

SAND PAPER

Great for breaking down fabric or leather.

ANYTHING SHARP

You'll need sharp objects for breaking holes in fabric.

ANYTHING BLUNT

You'll need blunt instruments for beating holes in fabric.

OIL

Lexol and mineral oil are my two favorites. Either use by themselves or in combination with Fullers Earth.

These are the basics. As we talk about aging things we'll get into all the various ways of using these materials.

Let's start with hats.

As every old-timer in costume design knows, when you're doing a Western, the hat is everything. Sometimes, when fitting extras, we'll fit the hat first — find the one that really works with the face — and then dress the rest of the outfit accordingly. I always like to take a lot of hats that have a "natural" shape, that is, the crown is fully rounded without creases, and shape it to the actor's face during the fitting. But the big thing is breaking it down, especially a new hat.

The easiest way is a little dangerous (for the hat). Fill a bucket with water and bleach. The more bleach you use the stronger the solution and the faster the action. Given enough time, a full bleach solution will eat a hat to pieces; so a gentle soak in a fifty/fifty solution will work slowly enough for you to keep tabs on it. The bleach will eat off the nap, and thin the "hand" (body) of the felt, as well as take out the color.

If you don't want to take it down that far, use shaving cream and a safety razor instead — and shave the hat. You will preserve the color, but by taking off the nap the hat will start looking worn. You can also work outside with a spritz bottle of water and bleach, squirting the hat and letting the sun help.

To help keep its shape, we always used to soak the hat in beer and water (an old cowboy trick), then shape it by hand and set it in the sun to dry. When the hat dries, the beer impregnates the felt and leaves it stiff, keeping the hat shape.

There are various ways to dirty a hat. If it's a straw hat, squirt it first, overall, with water, then lightly spray it with brown hair spray from about a foot away. When the brown looks like you've made a mistake, spritz it again with water. The brown tint will slide on the water and look like rain streaks. You can dab at it with a sponge or paper towel also, as this will further model the color. In fact, as long as you keep it wet, you will be able to get rid of most if not all of the brown tint. When you have it where you want it, fix it with a shot of either dulling spray or matte varnish.

If you're working with a felt hat, keep in mind that dark hats are very forgiving, but light-colored hats can retain mistakes. So go slow.

Start by making an "aging block." Melt wax in a pan. When it is fully liquid, add colored Fullers Earth and then pour the solution into a wax paper cup. When it dries, peel away the cup and what you have left is a block of aging color. Pre-made sticks are also sold at most costume house supply stores.

Now grind the colored wax into the felt body around the base of the crown of the hat. This is to simulate sweat. You might even want to paint on a "salt ring" with off-white paint and a fine brush. You might want to experiment with painting lacquer or varnish around the sweated area of the hat.

You can dust the hat with Fullers Earth too. Just pour the granulated color into a sweat sock or a double-folded square of cheesecloth, and tape or tie the open end shut. Hold this "pounce bag" over the hat and shake. The filtered color will drift down to cover the hat (simulated trail dust); then spritz with water (simulated rain); and set in the sun. As you're blocking (shaping) the hat, get your hands slightly dirty with a mixture of Fullers Earth and mineral oil and handle the hat the way you normally would while putting it on and off. Soon, you'll begin to see a lived-in hat.

Before we go any further, a cautionary note. Aging and distressing can ruin clothing. Be sure you know who OWNS the clothes you're working on and whether or not you're allowed to damage the clothes. By damage I mean making holes or using color that will not come out. This is especially true if you're using authentic and original clothing from a rental house. Remember, these old pieces have survived over time, and are now ready to support you on your show because of the care that a generation or more of costume people have given them. Please, don't destroy them out of lack of respect or through carelessness.

If you want to get something dirty without leaving permanent stains, use Fullers Earth only. Apply it with a whisk broom or a pounce bag, then brush it with your hand — light colors on dark and dark colors on light.

For larger jobs, or more permanent results, you need to start with a large, sunlit outdoors area. I always try to buy a galvanized horse feeder or large laundry tub. Fill the tub with water and Fullers Earth. Heat a pan of water and dissolve a couple of packages of tan dye, then add this to the Fullers Earth mixture. Stir the pot... then dunk the clothes, wring them out slightly, and hang them on double wooden hangers. I like to drape an old bath towel around the hanger first. This way the shoulder of the garment is softened at the edges and doesn't pick up hanger marks. You can throw things on the ground to dry also, turning them over to the sun.

If you want the garment to look old and droopy, put rocks in the pockets and then hang it up on a dress form and get it wet. Now you can spritz the top shoulder area, chest, center back and outer arms with a mixture of bleach and water to create some fading. Sometimes we cover a dress form with a plastic trash bag, then put the garment on that to work on. The aging looks more natural if it's done this way because of the body shape of the form, especially at the shoulder area.

While wet, the fabric will give differently; so now, hit the edges of the garment with a rasp, a file, a fish scaler — anything to break the fabric weave.

Let everything dry a little, remembering that the color will change when dry, to see where you are... then continue, until step by step, you have the look you want. If it looks too dark... hit it with a hose. When done, a lot of the Fullers Earth will return to powder and you will be able to brush a lot of the color out, but a nice tan patina will remain.

For a little extra character, look around elbows and knees, and find some fabric you like... then patch the elbow or knee hole from underneath. You can also use other fabric to bind the edges of lapels or cuffs. If you are adding patches, age them as you go so they look like the rest of the garment. If the patches are unaged, the garment will have a Raggedy Ann, clownish look (of course, that could be what you want).

Leather items are another story. If you're aging Indian clothing, a bath in a tub of Fullers and water will soften the color and give it a more "natural" look. It will accept aging from a grease rag too. But, if you're starting from scratch, you should go directly to a tannery and get the leather before they finish it. It's called a *natural finish*, or sometimes they call it a simulated smoked finish or a brain-tanned finish.

If you have to use leather that already has a "chromate" finish and you are making period or ethnic costumes that require a natural look, you might have to have the leather sandblasted first. This will break down the factory finish and open the leather to taking your dye and aging. So if you're trying to age a modern-made leather garment — coat, pants, chaps, etc. — get ready for a time-consuming and dirty process.

You first have to take the factory protective finish off the leather. This can be done with leather preparer, acetone, lacquer thinner, or paint remover. Always wear gloves and use a rag. On *The Last of the Mohicans*, we had so much leather, and the hides were so big, we would staple the cow hides to a piece of plywood and sandblast the chromate finish right off.

Once the finish has been removed, areas that have to show more use can then be sanded down deeper into the raw leather. From here on out it's up to the kind of finish that you're going after. The leather can be molded with color using alcohol-based leather dyes. A finish can be painted on and then sealed. Lacquer or varnish can stiffen and look crystallized. The best way is to leave yourself open and have something extra so you can experiment.

If you are going to use paint, ask at the paint store for information. Most large paint stores carry pamphlets and brochures on a variety of paint finishes and antiquing processes and products.

CHAPTER SEVEN

THE COSTUME DEPARTMENT SUPERVISOR

Once, while working in Spain with an English production staff, I had a conversation with the British UPM about his idea of show management. He always looked pretty relaxed, so I asked him his secret. "Well, I've hired the best, old boy. No use getting upset about things... after all, if you hire someone to do a job, then constantly tell them how to do it... well, it's like buying a dog and barking yourself." I laughed at his line but have always admired the truth of it.

If we view the costume department as a business, where costumes are made and used under the direction of a costume designer, then the position of supervisor can be likened to that of a general manager.

Whether you're working on a small or large project, the job requirements are the same. The only difference is the scale.

The general manager or supervisor carries out the BUSINESS of the department. It's this function that can come in conflict with the creative head, the costume designer. Who has the authority to hire and fire? Who can say what money will be spent where? In other words, who's the boss?

In Chapter 1, we talked about the working relationship between the designer and the supervisor. It's worth going over again from the perspective of the supervisor.

If a decision has to do with the look — that is, with the design, direct manufacture, selection of rentals or purchases, dying, trimming, etc. —

then the responsibility belongs to the costume designer. If it has to do with the physical organization of the department, Wardrobe labor, day-to-day set operations, the physical handling or moving of costumes (or the costs of any of these)... then it's up to the supervisor.

As I mentioned before, the final, overall department budget has to come from BOTH parties, because both parties will have different responsibilities that will have to be addressed before the department can function throughout the production period.

The designer is more of a professional artist, that is, that the designer has spent more time, thought, talent, desire, and inspiration to become proficient at the application of artistic and aesthetic principles in the medium of costumes — their history, symbolism, design, construction, coloration, and fit — as directly applicable to the visual format of motion pictures.

On the other hand, there is the physical job of organizing a department, which involves using physical help within a physical space, and using physical items of inventory to fulfill the task of supplying the production department with its scheduled requirements while keeping it informed of the inherent costs. This is all the job of the supervisor.

If you are the supervisor, you've been hired by a designer to supervise a show. Right away, if you have any doubts about what's going to be required of you or what your working relationship will be, talk about it over lunch. Figure out, between the two of you, how you want to split the duties.

Remember, the designer will always be looking for back-up. The designer feels the weight of production requirements, and may be a little unsure about the future. Designers know they're capable of doing the job... but the job can't be done alone. Designers can make the decisions about how a show should or could look. Designers aren't afraid of hard work... but they also know that they can't personally do everything. The question for you then as supervisor is: What's the best way to help the designer and the company, and yourself, all at the same time? The answer is: Make the department happen. Make it happen with good humor. Make it look easy. Make it happen with style.

Whether a big or small production, the job's main requirement is ORGANIZATION.

Here are the six areas that will always require your attention.

1. **PHYSICAL SPACE** This includes not only the space itself, but also fixtures, equipment, and amenities.

2. **LABOR** You will decide who works in the department, on what, and for how long.

3. **INVENTORY** This means keeping track of the costumes from accumulation through returns.

4. **SCHEDULE** Everything has to be timed to coincide with production needs and shooting.

5. **SET OPERATIONS** This includes the moving of costumes to locations, dressing of extras and cast, and monitoring day-to-day continuity.

6. **EXPENDITURES/FINANCES** You oversee the budget, and take responsibility for it.

Wow, it sounds like a lot....Yes, it is a lot. That's why they call the job COSTUME DEPARTMENT SUPERVISOR. The good news is that it's the same every time. Once you do it a few times you'll find that you can ANTICIPATE a lot of the problems before they happen. You'll develop your own system for dealing with the never-changing department requirements. You'll learn to delegate responsibility. After you do it successfully you can relax in your self-confidence (although don't relax too much, you know what will happen).

Let's start developing a system for a successful department operation by taking, one by one, the responsibilities that we've found to be constant.

The first thing you want to do after reading the script and making your breakdowns is to have a meeting with the designer and decide on department conduct and STRATEGY. You both have to develop a long-range plan for the management of your department. This is the first step in your partnership. A mutual understanding is critical.

Discuss where and how the costumes are going to be accumulated. Find out how the designer envisions doing the film; how much the designer wants to manufacture in-house; and how much and what kind of department work the designer wants to create.

Next, outline the phases of production (see below). Phase One, Preparation, is the time in which the costumes are to be accumulated, made, rented, and manufactured. This is naturally more the designer's time. Everything during this period is directed toward fulfilling the department's preparation needs under the direction of the designer, and this process will be managed by the supervisor.

After Phase Two, Moving to Location, Phase Three, Production, is directed toward fulfilling Production's requirements in maintaining a shooting schedule. Because this is the time for physically handling costumes, this is the period under the direction of the supervisor, and everything is supplied by the designer. This way, both can set up the prep: the designer gets the help necessary to accumulate inventory, while the supervisor has the time to set up preparations for the upcoming production phase.

When the production phase begins, the supervisor is prepared with the organizational skills needed to facilitate Production, so the designer can continue to devote time to preparation of costumes without being distracted by set or department management demands. This is good department strategy!

Now you both know what you have to worry about.

PHASE ONE: PREPARATION

1. Designer workroom space

2. Inventory warehouse and work space (for laundry, fittings, etc.)

3. Packing, shipping, and receiving

4. Office space

PHASE TWO: MOVING TO LOCATION

1. Truck

2. Container

3. Shipping boxes

PHASE THREE: SHOOTING DEPARTMENT

1. Workroom for alterations

2. Warehouse

3. Maintenance (laundry)

4. Extras' dressing area

5. Shipping/receiving

6. Office

7. Set truck(s)

PHASE FOUR: WRAP

1. Warehouse

2. Maintenance

3. Office

Now let's look at the job. The first thing is PHYSICAL SPACE. You can't work without it. Good space, well stocked with equipment and supplies will mean the difference between a marginal struggle and a great department.

In your budget breakdown, the designer's workroom requirements goes on a separate page. Estimate from the breakdowns how much inventory you have to warehouse and work during each production phase, and how you see the department operating, space-wise, during shooting. For this, you will need to get with Production and find out about the locations and the requirements for extras.

Line producers already know that you are coming. You and your department have been budgeted and are expected. They have a limited amount they can offer within their budget. Your job is to draw up a list of department job-related facility demands, then find out whether Production has anticipated the same hurtles you anticipate, and whether they are ready to give you what you need. Whatever the situation, from now on you will have two enemies: TIME and MONEY.

The time crunch is a problem that will never go away. You're in a race, where every shooting day is a finish line. You cannot afford to waste any time. Get a plan, agree on it, stick to it, make it happen. Your first priority is to help get the department up and running... that means getting the designer started.

Make a facility plan based on your anticipated workload and schedule. Next, list all the equipment that has to fill that space in order to bring the department alive. Phase by phase, area by area, job by job. What does the designer need? What do you need? What will it cost (or what can you use for a realistic allowance)? (All this information plugs into your budget package.)

For LABOR, follow the same sequence of events and jobs. Figure out who you need and when. The designer will want to figure out a personal help list based on experience and work type. Jobs might include: designer's assistant, sketch artist, shop foreperson, cutter-fitter, table lady, stitcher, milliner, and ager/dyer.

On the west coast, Costumers Local #705 is the union that handles Production contracts for the costume membership. I'd like to para-phrase job descriptions out of the union contract so you can see how Hollywood defines the areas of costume labor.

COSTUME DEPARTMENT SUPERVISOR
The costume department supervisor manages, supervises, and handles the general operation of the wardrobe department; has the responsibility to see that the department functions properly and is responsible for avoiding production delays; breaks down the script; may costume actors or actresses for shooting tests; acquires research material; fits and handles men's or women's wardrobe, as the case may be; is responsible for organizing the costume department and

hiring assistants, which includes shopping for and purchasing necessary costumes, renting costumes, finding costumes, and supervising the manufacture of costumes.

COSTUME DEPARTMENT FOREPERSON

The costume department foreperson manages, supervises, and handles the general operation of either the men's or women's wardrobe department, under the supervision of the department head. The foreperson shall NOT act as costume key person or as a costumer except in cases of emergency. Responsible to see that the department functions properly and to assist in avoiding production delays.

COSTUME KEY PERSON

The duties of a costume key person include the breaking down of the script, the shooting of tests, locating research material, and the fitting and handling of wardrobe, etc.

COSTUMER

The duties of a costumer are to assist as directed.

While these titles are in the union contract, they don't always represent the actual job titles that people work under on a show. For example, I don't remember ever working on a show where someone was designated as "foreperson." These job descriptions are written for the sake of pay-scale justification. When staffing a union show you have to figure out how much labor you need in each classification to do your labor budget. Most of the time you will want to start with a costume key person. If you're the supervisor, this person is your next in command. You want to find a person with experience on the kind of show you're going to do. Someone who has been there, seen the problems particular to the genre you're doing, someone familiar with the types of costumes, the fitting of extra crowds similar to the ones you expect (or larger) and to the scale of the location. You want to be able to huddle with this person and exchange ideas on how best to do things and know that your key understands the details of the job and what's expected.

If your show is large enough, you may have to split the duties — with you supervising from the department and the key running the set.

The rest of the wardrobe crew is decided by the size and type of show; some of the jobs might include:

SHACK MAN

That's what we used to call the person who runs the truck or the department. This person oversees the turnaround of used inventory as well as repairs, cleaning, and restocking. The shack man also helps with fittings for extras, and helps set up cast clothing during the day while the key set person is on the set.

KEY SET PERSON

This person will be devoted to the set and have no other department duties. This person sets up the cast changes in the mornings, and spends the day working the cast costumes to camera, including doing the continuity or matching (keeping "the set book" which is a complete logged record with notes and Polaroids of matching descriptions for every actor in every scene). If desired, the key set person works with the key costumer, after shooting, to transfer the day's continuity information to a master set book, which NEVER leaves the department.

SET PEOPLE

Additional costumers who help mostly with the background.

DEPARTMENT LABOR

Laundry person, local repair person, and an extra stock person to help the Shack Man.

In the old days we would sometimes divide the department up by costumes. One person took the men's civilian clothing as a "job" or area of responsibility for the whole show, while another took the women's costumes, another the cast, another the uniforms, and another took the ethnic costumes. On a day that was heavy with cast, we all pitched in and helped that person. We were all "swing" labor for each other. Nobody got too bossy and everybody helped everybody.

Sometimes we would split the work up by set. A couple of us would prep and pre-fit extras for the next set, while a couple of costumers were working on the set shooting now. We would leap-frog, being a help for each other in turn.

Again, go down your list of needs Phase by Phase. Every show is different, yet the same things have to get done. A sophisticated musical will staff differently than a large-scale war film, but the department process will be the same. The composition of your costume crew will be dictated by the difficulty of locations, the number of extras, expected damage to the clothes, and types of costumes handled.

Everyone's job revolves around the costumes. This is your INVENTORY. The only reason that any of us enjoy a living in this area is because of the clothes. Our value to any company, and our future career potential, is directly tied to our knowledge and ability in the care and use of clothing and costumes, theatrical and historical. As they used to tell me at Fox: "Rags are the department's life-blood, they're what's going to pay your bills and put food on your table... treat them with respect."

All the space and labor you plan for and budget for serve only one purpose: making these clothes look good on camera and getting the right ones there at the right time to best illustrate the story. If you realize them as your TOOLS, and give them that importance, then your decisions about their selection, transportation, storage, maintenance, organization, use, recovery, and return will be guided by respect, and therefore you will do your job better, and the overall project will be better.

To stay ON SCHEDULE, the idea to keep in mind is that you march to the beat of Production's drum; so everything you do is aimed at accommodating Production's time table. The good news is that Production can tell you the order in which the shooting will take place. Knowing this — especially on a short prep schedule or facing a large manufacture workload — allows you to work on the items needed for shooting first, and to continue prepping during shooting, so that you can still finish things in time for work later in the schedule.

SET OPERATIONS is what all the other work is about: "working the clothes to camera." As a supervisor, your key set person is the most IMPORTANT person on your crew. Why? Because the key set person is your department's direct representative on the set with the actors, continuity, camera, the First AD, and the director. You and your entire department will be perceived through the actions, dependability, personality, competence, concern, helpfulness, and all-around professionalism of this person. Also, this person is the eyes and ears of your department on the set. This person will be the first to receive any changes in schedule, cast, or anything else. This person will be in a position of close personal contact with every star member of the cast. This person will be responsible for monitoring continuity with the script supervisor, keeping the set book up to date, and keeping track of the many thousands of dollars' worth of cast clothing (often irreplaceable). As far as experience is concerned, I would give anyone a chance to do this job, for the first time, only if that person wanted it badly enough to take it seriously, and I had confidence in this person's understanding of professional set behavior. In fact, I would rather have such a new person, alert and determined, than someone who had done it a thousand times and didn't care or was lazy or distracted. As Dick James, the department head at Fox, used to tell me, "Kid, if you're going to take your show on the road, you better be up to speed!"

The work won't happen without EXPENDITURES. You will always have to face the money. You might start by reading a book on basic accounting. Develop a system for handling petty cash and purchase orders within your department, including cash, receipts, ledger book, and all. As supervisor, part of your job will be "disburser," that is, you will handle the finances of your department. Unless you have the luxury to delegate to someone else, you're it.

Some department heads enjoy this part of the job more than others, but the ones who do it best are the ones who address the department cash flow with the seriousness that it deserves. This goes hand in hand with your vigilance in continuously updating the department show budget. Your weekly meetings with the show accountant, who will see your department "cost report," will help you keep tabs on your expenditures.

Successful supervisors always have a network of vendors. People they find from show to show — suppliers, craftspeople, people they can use again and again. You realize that your ability to pull off a show might depend on knowing that outstanding hat maker or boot company. A network of vendors helps keep you independent and not too reliant on any one source for what you need. These are the relationships that you will keep ONLY IF THEY'RE PAID ON TIME. *Reminder:* Always walk vendor invoices through the accounting department, where, for any number of reasons, the accountant might not be disposed to paying that invoice promptly. I accept as my personal responsibility the job of getting my vendors paid. I never just leave the paperwork in a basket somewhere and hope for the best. The last thing you will ever want to hear on the phone from the only business you know that can help you, is "We sent you the stuff last time and we never got paid."

The more focused you become on mastering these six areas, the easier the job will become. Even the largest job, the biggest show you could ever think of, will still have these six areas to contend with... it's just a question of scale.

There's another dimension to the department that's always present, an important one to be sure, but one that most people never address. It's the EMOTIONAL DEPARTMENT.

A few of the sayings that ruled the old studio department were: "Never rat out the department"; "If you see your boss working, then you're not doing enough"; "Everybody's the enemy"; "If you're going to fool around on the show, keep it below-the-line"; and my personal favorite (which I mentioned earlier) "You can do anything you want, except two things: never be late, never make a mistake."

Working on a show on a long location with long hours and perhaps ugly weather (I still remember *Little Big Man*, shooting in Canada with a wind chill factor of 78 degrees below zero) can get everyone's nerves on edge. Like any close-knit family, sometimes tempers flare. What all those old department rules were saying was, whoever you are, wherever you are, YOU ARE the Department, a professional costume department. Work together, support each other, keep your problems to yourselves. Never bad-mouth the department to people outside the department. Never cross the line with too personal a relationship, because it causes unprofessional entanglements that can become divisive and destructive to your working relationships.

This is called DEPARTMENT INTEGRITY. Maybe times and conditions have changed and sensibilities say that's it's not possible to get a diverse group of people to sublimate themselves to the concept of an ideal wardrobe department... but it's important to try. It's healthy. It promotes a sense of well-being to know that when you go out to the set you won't be in trouble, and you won't be yelled at. You won't have to work in a panic all the time, because you can trust that everybody's doing their job.

Then one day the dailies look great, the cast and the extras are ready on time. Smiles all around, radio's on in the truck. You get to the set, that big crowd of extras you labored with this morning is in front of camera, and they look GREAT! The actors are playing the scene, relaxed... and they look great. You look around, the set person gives you a smile, it's all under control. The designer steps up, all the hard work is being shown off, right there in front of God and everybody, and you know at that moment that you have a GREAT DEPARTMENT... and YOU helped get it there... by getting everyone everything they needed to do their best... it's a proud feeling for everybody.

CHAPTER EIGHT

TIPS FOR GENRE FILMS

In 1997, I did a TV movie, The Broken Chain, *that was about the French and Indian war. The stunt people hated to wear the tight-fitting British tunics, so they took them off. The result... everyone in the shot was dressed in uniform except the guys that were getting blown up!*

WEATHER MOVIES   I have never worked on a "weather movie" but many of my friends have. Shows like *The Perfect Storm* or *Twister* are examples of films where the weather has a central part. Notice that when weather is a character, it's always BAD weather. These kinds of films require lots of multiples for cast changes and stunt doubles, as well as safety and weather gear for the crew. If your script reads with a lot of "weather action," plan on many meetings with the line producer and stunt coordinator about the amount of costumes and crew gear that you will have to supply, and the related costs of set labor, maintenance, repair, undergarments, wet or dry suits, hip waders, etc.

Something that might come in handy on any show is a DRYING ROOM. On *The Last of the Mohicans* it rained every afternoon. We had large crowds of extras every day, and by the wrap, the extras were always soaking wet. The problem was that they had to work the next day in the same matching uniforms or Indian outfits. Now if we took the time to break down all the outfits for the cleaners to dry overnight, it would have taken us hours, not to mention all the time needed to straighten all that out in the morning and rematch all the extras. The solution for us was to build a drying room. We built it in the basement of the wardrobe department out of the same materials that construction uses to build flats — basically door-skin and bat (1 x 3). We mounted eight-foot baseboard heaters on the floor along the walls and above them, and had chicken-wire shelves the length of the room. Each night, we collected the extras' clothing on rolling racks, each tagged with the extra's name and number, took them by truck to the department, rolled the wet clothes into the drying room, put the footwear on the shelves, and turned on the heaters (and a small exhaust fan). When we came back in the morning (six to nine hours later), the costumes were "baked" dry. The now-dry outfits were taken back to the set ready to re-issue, tagged and all.

WESTERNS These are usually a lot of fun. Beautiful outdoor locations, interesting people, and a chance to remake, in your own way, what has come to be the American classic genre. The downside is long hours, freezing mornings, roadside motel accommodations, wardrobe trailers full of dust and sand, light-fingered, souvenir-hunting extras, and second-unit stunt teams whose only job is fighting, getting shot at and falling off horses... in your clothes. So get plenty of multiples for cast clothing, as well as extra sets in triples — on shirts, hats, vests, pants, etc. Also, take plenty of stuff for the cast and crew: thermals, raincoats or ponchos, parkas, straw hats, and bandannas. Take a good supply of aging equipment. An expensive electric hat block is worth it if you have a big cast and are going to do a lot of hat fittings; along with a floor steamer to get those various blocks.

Speaking of hats...

As I mentioned earlier, I worked on a Western starring Dustin Hoffman called *Little Big Man* many years ago (1970). My friend and key set man was a costumer named Jimmy George. We were shooting on the CBS lot in Studio City, California, and the sequence involved an actor, Jeff Corey, who played Wild Bill Hickok. He was supposed to walk from his table to the bar. During his walk, a stunt man, at the back of the room, stood, hollered his name and drew a pistol. Jeff was supposed to turn, draw, and fire his pistol, killing the stunt man. We were cool, we had a dozen shirts for the stunt man, what could go wrong? During rehearsal it was obvious that Mister Corey could not draw his pistol fast enough to make it believable... so the director got an idea... have Jeff hold his pistol, at his side, inside his hat, on his walk, and when the stunt man yelled, Jeff would shoot his pistol, already drawn, through the top of his hat. Jimmy and I looked at each other in disbelief; we knew from experience that the director liked to shoot every sequence several times, starting with a wide angle master and getting progressively closer to the action, then doing reverses on each actor, which meant we might shoot this scene ten times. Now how many hats did we have? Two! This was going to be a bad day. All the rest of the wardrobe crew were at the costume house either prepping or returning; and these two hats had been custom-made for Mister Corey... we were not going to get more hats. What the heck were we going to do?

Well, we had to do something. We set a card table up behind the set. I got some cloth tape from our grip brothers and a pounce bag full of Fullers Earth that was closest to the hat color... and waited.

I could hear the set on the other side of the flat. "Action!"... "Blam!"... "Cut... get ready to go again"... then Jimmy's footsteps as he came around the corner with the hat, hole blown in the crown. I patched it from the inside with cloth tape, dusted the outside with spray glue and Fullers Earth and... "Blam!"... "Get ready to go again"... footfalls... new hat... tape, spray glue, Fullers Earth, "Blam!"... footfalls, hat... etc. How long this went on, I do not remember. What I do remember was hearing "Blam!" and the crew laughing while the director said "Cut"... Jimmy came back with a grin after the last take. When Jeff had shot through his hat, the whole crown had exploded in a shower of cloth tape, Fullers dust, and felt. The actors and director were laughing too. "Print, moving on." We had done it. What a relief!

MILITARY Just about everything you can say about a Western you can say for a military show, but it has its own quirks. Always take extra insignia, spray starch and an iron. Remember also that stuff gets heavy. I remember on *Tora! Tora! Tora!* (1970), we had over two hundred laundry hampers filled with military uniforms and equipment, shipped to Hawaii. When you fill a hamper (or now the more commonly used "E" container) with metal helmets, you have about two hundred pounds. The same goes for a container of leather boots, or canvas belt equipment, or wool overcoats and uniforms. Make sure you have plenty of muscle.

Even television movies like *Winds of War* were awash with every uniform from every army that fought in World War II. The sheer volume is staggering. The only thing that will help you on military shows this size is a dedicated sense of organization. Pigeonhole everything, get at least one person to devote themselves to learning, organizing, issuing, and reclaiming all the rank insignia, national devices, medals, ribbons, branch devices, etc. In other words, plan on having a separate insignia room within your military subdepartment, and get plenty of extra pieces.

Recently, I was asked to join the crew of the film *Pearl Harbor* (2001) as a technical advisor for the Japanese segment of shooting. My job was to go on location to Texas, where they had an aircraft carrier and were going to do the Japanese sequences prior to the attack on Pearl Harbor. Wardrobe had rented all the Japanese uniforms from Western Costume Company, and these were the same Japanese uniforms that were made originally for the movie *Tora! Tora! Tora!* Well, the funny thing was, standing on that carrier deck, watching all those extras wearing their Japanese uniforms, I realized that I had stood on another carrier deck some thirty-odd years ago, watching different extras do much the same thing in the SAME costumes. What comes around, goes around...

Now, think stunt department. Think of a stunt man, dressed in the uniform that you are using... now picture him throwing himself to the ground. Is he wearing a metal helmet? You might need to Vacu-form helmets for stunt safety. If there are metal canteens on the hip, stuff the canteen cover with soft foam. Stunt people will take off anything they think might be dangerous. Plan ahead. If it's part of the costume and you think it's going to break, take a few more.

While I was preparing this book, a friend of mine was hired to supervise a television pilot for a series about the war in Vietnam (mentioned earlier). It would have three weeks to prepare, and then shoot for about three weeks in Hawaii. The supervisor asked me to go with him as the person to be in charge of turning around the uniforms and helping to back up the department.

The script spent about half the time in the field and about half the time in a camp, a jungle fire-base. Everything sounded pretty straightforward.

Our meeting with the director was reassuring. He gave us the names he wanted on the name strips and told us that our extra count would never exceed twenty or thirty people in addition to cast. The supervisor wanted to go to the location ahead of time to survey our department and was told it wasn't necessary. The unit production manager assured us that we would have a department setup in an old, two-story house, which was on the location at the base camp area. We brought up the question of crew gear, and we were told that under NO conditions would Wardrobe have to purchase any water or safety gear for the crew, because each department would have to be responsible for its own needs.

We knew that the director was a Vietnam veteran himself, and that he wanted to have everything as accurate as possible. So we tried to look up and Xerox all the research we could on war photos and regulations, as well as purchase and take with us several books on the war. I have done a couple of other Vietnam films — *A Rumor of War* (1980) and *Hanoi Hilton* (1987) — and I have put up several others as an in-house costumer at various costume houses, so I felt very secure in my offhand knowledge of insignia and uniforms.

We assembled the costumes accordingly. We fit about half of the cast at the costume house; the rest, mostly day players, would be fitted on location. We packed the show for shipment, about twenty "E" containers (25" x 29" x 42").

The "E" containers were shipped with the property cargo container, and the supervisor and I got ourselves ready to travel to Hawaii. Hawaii is a beautiful place. Much of its beauty lies in the fact that it's so green... lush... tropical. It gets green and tropical because of the rain... lots of rain.

The company hadn't prepared for it, and despite its promises, hadn't given us any department space. The house they promised us went for office space to other departments who got there first. We finally got them to give us a forty-foot metal storage container in the middle of a muddy parking lot. The show turned into a constant fight against muddy clothes. When we started shooting, the director seemed to forget the conversations we had in town about what he wanted — and the extra count doubled and tripled. What should have been a run-of-the-mill shoot became a near disaster because the company hadn't thought to take the costume supervisor on a location scout (to see the location and make a plan ahead of time).

123

DANCERS   Dance movies seem to be a thing of the past, so not many film costumers have had a chance to work on them recently. Dancers have their own requirements. I've been fortunate to work on three or four shows with sizeable dance sequences — *1941* (1979), *Lost in the Stars* (1974), and *Hello Dolly!* (1969). The films were a world apart from each other. *1941* was a comedy about World War II, with a dance sequence in a USO canteen. *Lost in the Stars* was a musical take on the book *Cry, the Beloved Country*, about apartheid in South Africa, with dance sequences that were African-inspired and almost tribal, but definitely Hollywood choreography. *Hello Dolly!* was a real musical/dance/comedy, a story set in turn-of-the-century New York about a marriage broker. Now, on the surface, these three films had absolutely nothing to do with each other, and not a common story could be told... but, they all had dancers, and the problem that dancers have is the same, no matter what show it is.

Think movement.

In *1941*, about thirty couples were dancing a jitterbug/swing, with all the men in various uniforms, and all the girls in '40s cotton dresses. The set was an old dance hall with a wooden floor. The supervisor asked me to oversee this segment while they were shooting the film; so I started going to the dance rehearsals. The dancers rehearsed, first in their own clothes to get their moves... getting into the "swing" of things.

Everything at this stage was centered around the choreographer and developing the dance routine. I used this time to get the sizes of the dancers, measuring them myself, making size sheets out for everyone and taking their Polaroid picture. I made arrangements for a costume fitting as soon as I could pull the outfits together. After all, we had about month — four weeks until the sequence was to be shot, plenty of time... piece of cake.

Back at the department, I gave the photos to the supervisor who sat with the designer and decided which of the male dancers would wear what uniform, Army, Navy, Marine, and which of the women dancers would wear what dress. There were other, more immediate things that absorbed their attention; after all, we had an easy three weeks before the dancers worked on camera, and we already had the costumes, so what could go wrong?

Decisions came down, I got the costumes together, tagged them with the dancers' names and took them to rehearsal... so far so good. Shooting was a little closer... about two weeks away.

I had a fitting with the dancers. Everyone put their costumes on and they tried their dance routine, playback music and all. Words cannot express... everything, up until this point, had been perfunctory, easy, by rote; but now, suddenly, EVERYTHING WAS WRONG! The dancers couldn't wear this, the dancers couldn't wear that, they slipped, they couldn't raise their arms, they couldn't kick their legs. I was relieved of my complacency with consciousness-shattering abruptness. I had a problem. I had a lot of problems...

Think movement. The problems with the women's clothes were mainly with cap-sleeves. They couldn't raise their arms due to the inset and down angle of the sleeve opening. We fixed this by adding gussets to the underarms. Shoes were another problem. Their leather sole dance flats slipped on the wooden floor so rubber soles had to be added.

The men had it much worse. The uniforms of the period fitted tightly in the body, with small armholes. Army and Marine tunics were worn with three-inch leather belts, with open brass buckles. Gussets had to be added but they couldn't show when the arm was down; this meant that Spandex had to be dyed to match the uniform color and sewn in as gussets under the arm hole openings and in the crotches of the pants. Rubber had to be added to the bottoms of their service shoes. Leather belts with metal buckles had to go; in their place, softer vinyl belts with soft gold vinyl buckles were made and sewn down. Shirts had to be cut into dickeys to eliminate extra heat, and dance tails had to be added to the tunics to keep them from riding up during the routine. Sixty outfits, two weeks left, and I still had to have a final fitting. The bottom line is that in the end everything worked great... but we didn't have a moment to spare.

Lost in the Stars was a musical set in Africa. The major dance number was on stage at Fox: forty or fifty dancers in mock African outfits. The dance routine developed slowly, starting with the choreographer and dancers feeling their way through the routine. Suddenly the choreographer wanted all the dancers to have bells on bracelets and anklets as well as "nude" dance flats with rubber soles. All the jewelry had to be made — dozens of hoops with round Indian bells attached — another last-minute deal.

Hello Dolly! was an incredible experience. On the day of the big parade, shot on the Fox lot, we dressed *over five thousand extras* each morning. The parade itself wound back though the lot a half a mile; over a dozen horse-drawn floats, cavalry units, the Budweiser beer wagon drawn by twelve huge Clydesdale horses, interspersed with groups of marching bands. It was huge, grand, and everyone, crew and extras, were thrilled at the sight. At the head of the parade was the principal group of marchers, a fictitious Lodge unit. When the director called "Action," the parade started, and the whole line of horses, floats, and marching bands moved forward, through the narrow lot street between large sound stages, while the camera was raised on a crane. There was singing, there was music... the director yelled "Cut, everybody back to number one." Horse teams couldn't be turned in the narrow streets between sound stages and had to be un-harnessed, backed up and re-harnessed; heavy floats, built on real wooden wagons, some with circus animals, had to be pushed back into position — sometimes ten feet, sometimes fifty feet, by hand. Shooting this sequence took the better part of a week... by the end of shooting, the thrill was gone for everyone.

The dancers we had all experienced the same problems discussed before — gussets, four-way stretch clothing, and leather sole shoes. These are the normal problems for dancers, so if you have them in your shoot, check with the choreographer early.

The other big challenge of *Hello Dolly!* and a requirement that comes up regularly on many shows is dressing large crowds of extras. Dressing that many street extras required some thinking; changing time was a concern, and so was the number of costumes that could be rented. The solution: dickeys. The male extras were called in their own dark suits. Cheap cardboard hats, like the kind found in amusement parks, were bought, and dickeys were made from shirt fronts, velcroed at the back of the collar, with ties and vest fronts sewn down. Tie strings were attached to the bottom sides of the shirt fronts. The extras came in with T-shirt only, and the dickeys could be put on in mere seconds under their coats; the cheap hat graced each head and off they went. The women didn't get away that easy, but black elastic or drawstring waist skirts, white shirts, dark coats or shawls, and large, dark hats, streamlined the dressing time and made the background blend in.

Oh yes, we dressed about a thousand of the above extras in period clothes to line the streets for the main shots to screen the background extras.

NATIVE AMERICAN SHOWS I've had the pleasure of working on several films and television shows about Native Americans, including *Little Big Man* (1970), *When the Legends Die* (1972), *The Return of a Man Called Horse* (1976), *The Broken Chain* (1993), *Tecumseh: The Last Warrior* (1995), *Geronimo* (1993), *Crazy Horse* (1996), *Stolen Women* (1997), *Miracle in the Wilderness* (1991), and *The Last of the Mohicans (1992)*.

The main problems are ones of cultural understanding. Many people don't realize that the Native American long house way of life is still alive; that many traditional Native American families raise their children in the old way, with respect and quietness, where certain objects are still considered sacred, such as eagle feathers.

On *Crazy Horse*, we had some headdresses that were very old studio pieces, made or bought in the days long before eagle feathers were illegal to own under The Endangered Species Act. I thought that having them would add a certain something to the film, which painted turkey feathers lacked. I didn't anticipate the mixed reaction I got from the Sioux extras. Some were taciturn enough, but some expressed their discomfort at using sacred items in a film, and having them handled by non-native actors. They would NOT let my women costumers touch the feathers AT ALL! They considered this to be extremely disrespectful. In the end, I was sorry I took them.

Since then, I've found that a great-looking mock–eagle feather comes from the peahen. The peahen's tail feathers are longer than a turkey's and naturally have a dark and light mottled pattern that resembles the eagle.

CHAPTER NINE

THE SHOOT

Costume design is always a collaborative effort. I found that working with a variety of talented designers has been one of the most educational aspects of the business. The shoot for the feature film Little Big Man *was full of challenges. The locations were beautiful, and Montana and Canada were interesting to be sure — getting close to the Crow tribe, enjoying their powwow songs and dances, visiting the buffalo reserves, seeing those big beautiful animals in person, and seeing the grandeur of Banff National Park. But that's not what stands out in my mind. What I remember most was the weather. When we started shooting in Montana in July, it got up to 112 degrees on the prairie... day after day of it; and when we finished shooting in Canada in January, it hit 78 below (with the wind chill factor). I haven't been back to the snow since.*

The primary objective of the department during the production phase is supplying costumes for the camera according to the shooting schedule. All the design and department preparation work is aimed at this objective: getting everything in front of the camera to be photographed.

I'm going to describe an average shooting day. Because everybody is working at the same time, I'm going to follow one job for a while, and then back up and discuss another.

As supervisor, a normal location day might be something like this: You start at 4:30 or 5:00 a.m. Load your crew out of their motel rooms and into the department car or van for your drive to the set. When I was crew, I took this opportunity to sleep; but when I was supervising I took this opportunity to talk the day's schedule over with the key. We would map out a plan for our labor. What was on the call sheet for the day? What department work had to be done? What did we still have to do to prep an upcoming scene? And were there any other problems we had to think about or deal with, including hiring and firing? When we got to the location and opened the truck we had a pretty good idea of what to do first.

The two main jobs in any morning are: 1) getting the actors' dressing rooms set up with the right clothes for their first change, and 2) getting the extras dressed and to the set.

We would always have the crew split. The key set person would go straight to the cast section, check the call sheet against the set book for matching, pull the cast changes that work first and start setting them up, getting them ready to go to the dressing rooms. This early in the day on the location is quiet. The shooting crew isn't here yet — just some drivers, maybe a second assistant director, someone from casting with the extras, and hair and makeup people. It may be too early even for the catering truck. Without distractions, those of us who aren't getting the cast changes ready for their imminent arrival are setting up to issue clothing to the extras.

So the key set person goes straight for the cast clothing. We always used the last rack in the truck on the right-hand side for cast clothing. We put their clothing on the high racks for storage; this was to keep principal clothes out of reach and sight for anyone who was not in the department, and also to keep the dead storage up and out of the way.

After checking the call sheet, the key set person pulls down the working clothes and lines them up on the lower prep rack.

On a new location, we would check with the Second AD as to where the rooms were for each actor. It's Production's job to assign dressing rooms and trailers. When we knew which actor was in what room, we would bring over the clothes and set up their rooms. Regarding setting up actors: We were always taught to put only the clothes in the room that work, i.e., the ones you want them to wear. If you ever put extra clothes in their rooms, even hidden in the closet, you will, one day, find a cast member wandering around asking "What do I wear?" When you say that you put the first change out and the later change in the closet, the actor will tell you that it was too confusing. The other thing they taught us was always to lay the change out in a "mistake-proof" fashion; that is, put the tie around the collar, put the cuff-links in the shirt, put the belt in the pants, put the socks on top of the shoes. Lay everything out extremely neatly, so that the actor has only to put the change on and not think about it.

If the actor has a lot of makeup to get into, provide them with a T-shirt, or a foundation garment and robe. This lets actors get into their costumes after makeup, saving the collar from soiling. Remember to take with you to the set what you don't think the actors will wear, such as overcoat, hat, gloves, etc. This will save you from running back to get them later.

BACK AT THE TRUCK   If we knew we had a "big extra day" coming, we would always try for a pre-fit day, fitting all the extras and having any alterations done in advance. Sometimes that's not possible for one reason or another. If we can't get the extras ahead of time, we try to put up outfits, by size, in advance. This way, you can keep the pieces together that you like, and see that they go out as outfits.

There are several ways to control extra crowds. You need to create a system that promotes order and helps you recapture the clothes as efficiently as possible. One way is to use sign-out sheets. Sign-out sheets can be any size; we used to have them about 18" x 24" but you can make them any size you want. Number down the left-hand margin. If you have a hundred extras, then you need a hundred numbered lines. When the extra comes for clothes the FIRST time, write down the person's name and make out a tag with the corresponding number. That number stays with that person for the entire show. You take the pay voucher, write the number on it, and file it in a box. When the extra is fitted, each is told to "go to the dressing area, put on the costume, hang your own clothes on the hanger, pin YOUR numbered tag to your clothes, and bring your clothes back to the wardrobe area."

When extras return with their clothes tagged with their numbers, you hang their personal clothes in consecutive order in your department. This way, during the day, they can't take off with your clothes and their

131

clothes too. At the end of the day you reverse the process. They come to the department, retrieve their clothes by number, change, return their costume with their numbered tag on the sleeve. If they return complete, you give them back their pay voucher, hang their outfits in the department in consecutive order and hope that tomorrow morning they will remember their numbers.

You will want to have laundry bags waiting at the truck to receive their socks, T-shirts, stockings — whatever is washable overnight. There are many variations on this system. Sometimes they leave their personal clothes on racks in the changing area. Sometimes you will want to write down the items that constitute their outfit; how ever you do it, the reason is the same: Control the clothes.

You will be amazed that people can find so many odd ways to put clothes on hangers. That's why we always found that it's best to have someone from the department circulate in the dressing area while the extras are getting changed. This strategy does several good things: You're able to help those who need help, and by so doing, you can establish a rapport with them in general. Your presence also helps deter those light-fingered souvenir hunters. The same is true for the line of extras returning costumes to the truck. Someone should walk the line, offering hangers, pins, and help in getting outfits ready to be received. It saves a lot of time at the truck when everybody wants to go home after a long day.

BACK TO THE SET Procedures will vary from person to person and show to show, but the main outline of a day's set work will, based on my experience, stay the same.

As a key set person, I would always check first with the first assistant director and make sure that the call sheet, issued the night before, was still good and reflected the order that was planned for shooting that day. Sometimes ideas are thought up after the call sheet comes out, so you won't know the changes unless you ask. If the First AD ever told me that they had added shots from another day that weren't on the call sheet, I would check the matching notes in my set book, then let the supervisor know what the changes were. Then the truck crew could make sure that the costumes needed were available, and not at the cleaners, being repaired, or being stored off-location.

They always told me that the best set people were the ones who understood that their job consisted of two parts: 1) keeping track of and working the cast clothing to camera; and 2) constantly keeping ahead of the company with information. This means always finding out what the company is going to shoot next, and keeping the department notified so that the department is always in a position to get a jump on preparing for an upcoming changed scene.

In the first set job I had at Fox, the department head, Dick James, told me: "Get your kit, and sit right under the camera; if they tell you to move, tell them that you have to see what the camera sees because you have to match it." And that's exactly what I did. I had my "set kit" (needles, thread, scissors, toupee tape, leather punch, etc.) in a wooden fishing tackle box. My first day on the set, I put my box right in front of the camera and sat down. The camera people were amused, and told me to "lighten up a little and get out of the way." My answer was "Nope, my department head told me to sit here and that's what I'm going to do." Everybody got a laugh out of my naiveté, but that's where I sat, and everybody soon got used to it. Later I learned that you can see what's going on without sitting under the camera lens; but this experience taught me to stay tuned to the shot so that I could always be watchful for those collars that poked out, buttons that weren't open, etc. Dick James also told me, "If it's no good for Wardrobe, it's no good for anybody." So if I saw a mismatch I would always dash onto the set between the last rehearsal and the first shot, and fix, change, or brush the costumes so that they matched, looking the way the supervisor wanted them. I would always check with the camera operator to find out what was in frame, and I always got to look for myself. This gave me a realistic idea as to what the camera saw, and I would know better what to do accordingly.

On the first day of shooting, I would always check in with the script supervisor and compare breakdowns. We always wanted to make sure that our breakdowns matched with regard to how many "story days" there were and that the "day breaks" were at the same scene numbers. The script supervisor matched everything in the scene except wardrobe (although once in a while some did, especially if a wardrobe gag was happening as part of the action). The script supervisor would always tell me, "Look, I have too much to keep track of already. You have to match the clothes." And of course I would anyway, because that was my responsibility in the department already.

At the start of each day I would sit with the call sheet and set book and figure out which actors would have to change clothes during the day for what scenes, and what the changes were. I would line up those changes on the truck or trailer to make sure that they were there, and then go to the set. During the day, when I saw that we were getting close to a scene where an actor was to change, I would tell the First AD so they would know to break. When they did break, I would go set up the next change. After the actor had changed, I would collect the last change, making sure that it was all there, and return it to the department. I was always told NEVER to leave clothes unattended in an unlocked trailer. (That's not true if you're using a "honey wagon," where the driver is always close. But remember, at the wrap, those drivers are in a hurry to leave, and will want you to get those rooms empty as fast as possible.)

I would try to remember to take things like actors' coats and hats to the set, lest they arrive without them after makeup, meaning I would have to run back out to the trailers to get missing pieces. I would do this also when lunch was called, because sometimes actors can get busy, and they leave their things on the backs of chairs or who knows where.

We always had rolling clothing racks at the studio on stage, so I always had a portable department to keep anything that wasn't being worn. Out in the field, where little rack wheels won't go, I always borrowed a "C" stand from my grip brothers for a stationary place to hang clothes, always making sure to return it (right to their truck if I could).

When the director got to the set, I would always say "good morning" and stand close enough to hear the director lay out the shots with the First AD and Camera. When I was satisfied that there weren't going to be any changes, I would turn my attention to the actors who were arriving on the set from makeup, making sure that they had their outfits, and that they hadn't left anything in their rooms or in the makeup department.

The next thing to watch is the rehearsal. Watching the actors run through their lines during rehearsal can be worthwhile, since this is where the scene blocking is taking place and where "wardrobe gags" might be developed. Actors also might be taking off hats or coats, there might be unanticipated physical action, or the director might decide on a piece of wardrobe for set dressing. After the rehearsal, the electricians and grips will take time to light the scene, so there will be time to prepare for anything new that came out of the rehearsal. Many times the lighting gaffer or the First AD will be able to tell you approximately how much time they plan on before they will be ready for a "camera rehearsal." This is the time when the actors will go back to makeup, back to their trailers, or they will join the director for a line reading. This is also the last time for a little touchup, if necessary, before shooting.

For the designer, there are no rules. The designer has to be where the designer has to be. Some mornings, especially the first morning of a costume change for an actor, the designer will probably want to be making sure that the clothes fit right, that accessories are there, that the hair and makeup people have any pertinent information and/or hair trimming pieces that will be used.

If the cast is set, the designer might want to oversee the dressing of the extra crowd, making sure that the background characters are as they want them. As everything starts moving toward the set, the designer will want to go there also, together with the supervisor, whenever possible.

Most directors and First ADs want the designer on-set in the morning, especially on days when a cast member is working in a new change. It's good politics also, making everyone comfortable with the fact that Wardrobe is represented on the set at the beginning of each day.

As designer, I would always hand-carry my favorite background jewelry or women's hats, or any "special" pieces to the set, rather than put them on the extras in the morning. Upon arriving at the set, I would query the set person about the action and blocking; then I would work with the second assistant director in the placing of background extras. I always felt that I could make a contribution here, since I'd just seen the extras get dressed and had a good idea of the better-looking "character" types. After placing the extras to camera and seeing where and what the shot was, I would then pass out the better pieces of costume jewelry and clothing so that they'd be sure to get into the film.

If the cast were new, then I'd be sure to show the director the new change. Most of the time, there had been so much communication about everything already that everything was fine, but sometimes something would have changed — perhaps a replaced actor — and there would be a little last-minute scramble to get things right.

If the cast were already set, then I would spend time with the extras, making sure that everyone was "done up."

On-set, the designer and supervisor can have a look at everything together. If the designer has any criticism about the way the extras look, the supervisor can fix things with the costumers taking care of the background.

BACK AT THE TRUCK The supervisor's department work day starts: Clean-up after the extras' fitting. Laundry out. Laundry back from the cleaners has to be hung, sized, and returned to stock. There are as many ways to organize stock as there are people doing it; but the main thing is to keep things together. There's nothing worse than to find something you want to use, then buying or renting it, taking it on location with a desire to see it in a certain scene, and then when that day comes... you can't find it. You've lost the opportunity... only to find, when doing returns at the end of the show, that exact piece hanging where it shouldn't have been. As they used to tell me: "If you can't find it, you might as well not have it."

We always would separate men's clothing from women's and children's. Depending on the type of show and the nature of the stock, you might want to separate the costumes by civilian and uniform, and then perhaps by civilian type — workers, townspeople, and better dress; or perhaps by set — saloon, bus station, etc. No matter what system you choose, whatever quiet time you have can be spent perfecting it. Put everything in size order. Check boxes to make sure that the contents are what you think. Check the stock to see if anything needs cleaning or repairs, and to discover things you can use on upcoming characters.

When it comes to sizing clothes, we always screwed a yardstick down to the edge of a counter, or used clear tape over a measuring tape for a size guide. (For complete size conversion charts, see Appendix.) Men's coats are sized under the arm hole with the coat laying flat on the yardstick. The trick to sizing is knowing how the garment is intended to fit. For example: a military jacket, which has to fit snugly, is measured seam to seam. A sport coat or suit coat, which has some play, is measured two inches down in size (about the length of your last thumb joint); this takes out about four inches. An overcoat might have four inches per side taken out, leaving room for a suit underneath.

Pants are measured by hooking up the front and placing the waistband on the yardstick. Whatever it measures, double it; that's the waist size. The other measurement is the inseam; that's the distance along the seam, inside the pant leg from the crotch to the bottom of the cuff.

A dress shirt is measured for: neck opening, button to button hole; and sleeve length, center back collar band to end of cuff.

Loose-fitting sport shirts can be measured across the chest and tagged with the inch measurement or "L," "M," and "S."

Women's clothes should always be sized by inches and not by dress sizes — 2, 3, 4, 5, 6, 7, etc. These measurements are very undependable in that they have changed over the years, and are not standard now in many instances.

Once arriving at the size, it is written on a shipping tag, sometimes with a code for the type of garment (e.g., a men's suit tag might read, S.B. 4-B 3PC., for single-breasted, four-button closure at coat front, three-piece with vest) because once a costume is hung in stock, only the sleeve will be visible.

When tagging a garment, always use a safety pin, which can be removed without tearing, and pin the tag through the button hole at the cuff or to the inside lining; this will create uniformity and lessen the damage to the sleeve material.

Hats, when pinned to outfits, should always be pinned through the inside hat band in the back. (A pin through the hat brim will create holes and damage; a pin through the front of the hat band will result in a rough spot that will hit an actor right on the forehead.)

Every show prepares to the very end. There are always things that need work, or fittings for late-arriving cast members, or getting ready for the next extra crowd — not to mention the paperwork and budget meetings. When you start to wind down, you can start the wrap.

The two big differences between a Movie of the Week and a feature are the inside prep time, and the size of the finished product. A feature will have its challenges of scale and detail (remember, you will see a shirt collar ten feet tall). But once you get into a set or sequence, you will usually have some time before the next set works, and that time is prep time. On a Movie of the Week, on the other hand, the pace is faster, with large sequences sometimes done in a day or two. Here, the prep time is shorter between sequences, and the costumes are turned around faster. The saving grace is that MOWs are more about the actors saying their dialogue; so, usually, as long as the people directly on camera are acceptable, you're covered. The background isn't as critical, since it just isn't seen as much because of the smaller screen size.

The shooting day ends with everyone recapturing the clothes. Extras are checked in, and costumes checked for missing items and cleaning. Cast clothing is returned to the truck, and checked for cleaning and repairs.

The last thing is to go over the advance call sheet for the next shooting day and make sure that all is ready for the morning.

If everyone is on weekly time cards, you can keep a weekly hour calendar, recording arrival, lunch, and finish times on a daily basis, which will eliminate those Saturday-night conversations that consist of questions like "What time did we go to lunch on Monday?"

Of course, every type of show has its own quirks. For instance, intensive stunt shows have their own unique requirements. On shows where there's a car crash or some other lone stunt, the work of fitting, rigging, or dealing with safety equipment can be done by the set crew. But action shows, Westerns, and war dramas can be a separate challenge. If your show is going to be stunt-intensive, you might consider a separate crew of one person or more just to take care of the stunt people.

A stunt person's first concern is safety. The second concern is working as quickly as possible. Wardrobe is not really important per se, it's just something they have to deal with in order to get in front of the camera.

Some common stunt items might include:

- **A CABLE RIG** of some kind, where a corset-like garment is worn. The corset has metal studs protruding, so that cables or wires can be attached, enabling the stunt man to "fly." After the costume is put on over the corset, holes have to be cut in the clothes to make room for the cables.

- **A JERK-OFF RIG**, similar to the cable rig. Used a lot in Westerns. A harness is worn on the upper body with a ring in the center back. After the coat is put on, a hole is cut in the back and the cable attached. For instance, the stunt person rides a horse toward camera, reaches the end of the cable, and is jerked off the horse.

- **STUNT PADS** are worn by all stunt people in general. These consist of forearm, elbow, shin, knee and hip pads. Hip pads are worn in an elastic waist girdle. These are common sports items and found at sporting goods stores. When worn they will take up extra room under any garment, meaning larger waist sizes and sometimes larger sleeve or pant leg widths.

- **BURN GAGS** consist of the stunt person being set on fire. This is the most dangerous of stunts. No one wants to see anyone get hurt here. If you have a burn gag in your show, be sure to discuss this with the stunt coordinator ahead of time. Costume doubles may have to be fire-proofed ahead of time. The stunt coordinator may want to avoid outer garments, made of synthetic fibers, that melt.

- **SQUIBS** are the most common device used on stunt people. Squibs are handled by the special effects crew. A squib is a small round metal dish fitted with a light explosive charge behind a prophylactic filled with stage blood. It is taped into clothing using heavy-duty fabric tape; wires are then run from the explosive charge, down pant legs to an electric board. When Effects makes contact on the board, the charge fires, blowing the stage blood through the clothing. To be sure that the charge gets through the fabric, the back of the clothing is sometimes scored with a razor blade. This usually leaves a large cross-shaped rip, about four inches by four inches, in the garment.

Of course, any of these stunt rigs is hard on costumes. When possible, the set person should try to help the stunt team rig for a stunt where holes are going to be cut in clothing. With a little effort, sometimes clothing seams can be opened instead of cutting holes in the body of the garment, helping to preserve the costume and save on later loss and damage costs.

Just a note on stage blood. If liquid soap is added to the blood, it will come out easier. Sometimes Effects will tell you that their blood is "washable," and indeed sometimes it is. However, it doesn't hurt the look of the blood to add a little liquid soap, and it's good insurance.

Rambo III was an action picture that took me around the world. We shot for months — most of the time two units, sometimes three. At every location Rambo would engage in shoot-outs with the Russian army. We had dressed the rank-and-file Russian soldiers in camouflage jumpsuits, and on the big stunt days we would shoot the same ten, fifteen stunt men, over and over and over. The effects crew wanted fifty coveralls on their truck at all times in order to pre-rig the insides with squibs. Fifty coveralls was a lot to me, as I had sometimes fifty extras dressed, plus the stunt team in multiples, which all had to be cycled through a day's laundry and repair service.

The solution? We parked a small five-ton truck next to the effects truck. In it, we had a sewing machine and all the stunt clothing. Next to the truck we had galvanized tubs filled with water, and between trucks we strung a clothesline.

We would hear the gunshots from the set. The bloody stunt crew would come to the wardrobe truck. We would undress them. They would use the water from one tub to wash up while we pulled the dead squib rigging out of their coveralls. We threw the squib rigging back into the effects truck for them to re-set, while the bloody coveralls were rinsed in another tub, then hung to dry. The stunt team then drew another, freshly rigged set of coveralls from the effects truck, and headed back to the set. The dry coveralls came off the clothesline and went to the sewing machine to be repaired, after which they would be given back to the effects crew to be pre-rigged for the next shot. This went on for weeks and weeks. By the time we were through shooting, the coveralls were a solid mass of zigzag repair lines. Why didn't we get more coveralls? In the beginning we had the simulated Russian camouflage material specially printed in the states at a commercial printer with a large minimum order; at this stage, we were shooting in Israel and our lines of communication made it difficult to engineer the project by phone; besides, what we were doing was working okay, and I had other more important things in my budget.

That Vietnam pilot in Hawaii had its own set challenges. The almost-constant rain and mud on the set required that lots of extra clothing be on hand; so in addition to the main department at base camp we racked a five-ton truck and parked it close to the set. That proved to be too far at times, so Production gave us one of the set buildings as an on-site mini-department. It was close and convenient, but due to lack of security we experienced unnecessary losses. Inclement weather increased production requirements in other ways; one night I got a call from the set to find a twenty-four-hour building supply outlet, and buy all the rubber overboots I could find. Another time I got a late call for wetsuits for actors. I was glad I had a car, a phone book and a map, because I used them every day.

CHAPTER TEN

THE WRAP

Back to our Vietnam show. We wrapped about three o'clock Thursday morning in the rain, heaps of wet and muddy clothes, heaps of wet and muddy costumers. The UPM (unit production manager) wanted us to throw everything in boxes and leave the island by Saturday, Sunday at the latest.

Our discussion followed familiar lines. We had to clean everything, sort everything, dry everything, separate and mend everything, then pack everything for shipment....Okay, so could we take Sunday off and have everything ready to ship by next Wednesday? Yes, we would try.

We came in later Friday and got out the cleaning. Saturday we cleaned muddy boots. Monday we started repairing the clothes that were clean and packed what we could. The way things were spread out we weren't going to get an inventory; the UPM said he didn't care, we would have to figure it out back in L.A.

Tuesday everything got packed. We were told that everything was to be shipped by barge, and would take a week to get back to L.A. We told the UPM that if that were the case, it would result in the clothes (boots especially) getting mildewed... which would have to be another thing we would have to sort out in L.A. Wednesday the boxes were put in a container for shipment anyway.

As luck would have it, we met the container met in L.A. the week of Thanksgiving. The UPM didn't want to pay us for the holiday, so we were told to start the unpacking and wrap after another week. We were given only a week to wrap. In that time we would have to make all the returns to four costume houses, etc.

When we came back to those boxes and unpacked them, there were over two hundred pairs of very mildewed boots. There was no way that the two of us could clean these boots and do the rest of the return, so, we had to hire two additional people for a week to clean the boots. We also had to send out much of the hanging stock to the cleaners for the same reason.

When the returns were complete, we were presented with a bill from one costume house for over sixteen thousand dollars in loss and damage for missing items. We were astounded. In checking the bill we found that the policy of this house was to charge ten times the amount of the rental for any losses. On the bottom of most rental contracts there's a stipulation that they CAN charge up to ten times the rental price, but most houses charge a reasonable amount based on whether the items missing are easily obtainable or not. In this case, war surplus would normally be charged at the purchase price plus a house fee of 20 to 35%. A pair of boots that retails for twenty-five dollars might cost thirty-five dollars... But we were being charged two hundred and fifty dollars a pair based on a twenty-five-dollar rental.

So I spent another week on payroll rounding up missing pieces. I spent about twelve hundred dollars and satisfied sixteen thousand dollars in loss and damage charges.

As the end of shooting moves closer, you get closer to the last big job — the return of all the rented costumes and the disposition of all purchases.

You will have only two types of inventory in the department: "yours" and "theirs."

I have been on shows that had ample wrap time and shows that wanted everyone off the clock the day after shooting; but no matter how much or how little time you have, the job of wrapping the department stays the same.

Wrap time should have been figured into your first budget and discussed with the line producer from the beginning, taking the following into consideration:

- **ONE** *What's the last thing we shoot?* Often times, the show will finish with stage work, pick-up shots or other small scenes. If this is the case, then the last weeks or days of shooting can be used as wrap time. Whatever isn't working can be cleaned, mended, sorted, and packed. If, however, the last days of shooting are large-scale, and your crew is engaged in handling the set, then that same amount of labor effort for cleaning, sorting, mending, and packing, will have to be done after the company wraps in the week(s) following production.

- **TWO** *How much will it cost?* The biggest expense after shooting will be dealing with the rental houses' charges for what THEY have to do to get your clothes back into their stock. If you don't sort things out because your labor is cut off, then the costume house will have to sort things out at THEIR labor cost. If you don't clean and mend your rented clothes, then the costume house will clean and mend at THEIR labor cost. If you have rented items that are missing or damaged and don't make an effort to replace them with items that your company owns, then you will be billed for the FULL REPLACEMENT PRICE. In some cases, these are in-house tailor-made prices, or up to TEN TIMES the amount of the rental. It's good to remember that when you rent anything, you are BORROWING someone else's things for a price; that business has a right to expect that you treat THEIR things with professional respect, and if you don't, you have the right to expect that they will charge you for it. The way to minimize loss and damage charges when returning rented costumes is simple; return things in the same condition they were in when you took them.

The ideal wrap would go something like this:

After shooting has finished, all costumes would be sent out, cleaned and returned to the department. (Sometimes this won't work. If your location is somewhere where there isn't a cleaners, or the small-town cleaners can't remove the blood, aging, or makeup in your clothes, the costume rental house will have to clean them again anyway. Also, remember, if

145

you clean the clothes, pack them and ship them back to their point of origin, and they arrive crumpled from being packed and thus are unsuitable to rehang in the costume house's stock, the costume house will have to send them out again for a steam and press; so you might want to check with the rental house first to come to some kind of understanding on this.)

The costumes are then checked for repairs, and any damages to the clothes are corrected. This usually entails a sewing machine and hand repair. When the rental house accepts their clothes back they are always checked for ill use and billed accordingly, so mending garments, cleaning and stuffing shoes, and steaming hats, while a bit time-consuming, pays off against L/D charges.

The clothes are then sorted by costume house. Most houses stamp their name inside the garments; sometimes the stamps look the same. Most (but not all) rental houses will refuse items returned to them that are stamped from another costume house. This will cause you problems if at the end of your shoot you return things to three or more places, only to have one or two of them call you later and tell you that you have losses with them plus returned clothes that aren't theirs, since this means you'll have to make another round and try to get the right pieces to the right places.

Once separated by costume house, the clothes are assembled according to billing sheet. This process is actually made harder with computer sheets, so a lot of costumers are demanding itemized sheets as well as computer inventory billing. If you have rented according to group, such as "Cowboys/Indians," the assembly is easier. The items are then tagged with the sheet and the line number corresponding to its billing sheet. This way the show's rentals are being assembled in reverse and when you're done, you will know ahead of time where your losses are and be able to make preparations to make, purchase, or somehow make substitution or payment for them. This works to the advantage of your company because it allows them to consider their options in advance so they won't be blindsided by a late and unexpected bill for loss and damage from a forgotten vendor.

Now your show can be packed for shipment home. Sometimes I've used TV boxes, filling each one with items from one sheet and writing the sheet number on top. Sometimes the clothes are returned in a truck or "E" containers; either way, if they are returned according to sheet number, the shipping department at the rental house can check in your show more quickly with less labor, and your final billing will be arrived at faster.

Finally, items that your show owns that you want to trade for loss and damage should be dealt with last, face to face, based on what the rental house knows about the losses and damages and any extra rental time.

The Production office will expect you to finish up the billing with them. All last-minute expenses — repair, purchase, cleaning — should be settled with the show accountant. When this is done, you are free to take a deep breath... and look for your next job.

Well, "that's a wrap," as we say. I hope that reading this book has given you some real insights and a few laughs.

I wish that there had been a book like this for me to read when I first entered the business. The information contained herein is an accumulation of thirty-five years of experience, a lot of it difficult. Maybe this book will make it a bit easier for you.

The film business is a great business. The experiences, personalities, conditions, creativity, opportunities, and challenges are unlike those found in any other field. It's one of the best-paying areas of employment to get into, and it offers plenty of travel and glamour. There are only two things you can't do: Never be late and never make a mistake.... Good luck with your future success.

APPENDIX

The following chapter contains names and addresses of costume houses, an assortment of sketches, and samples of breakdown forms previously discussed.

The following list is in no particular order, and is (of course) only a partial list of costume houses worldwide.

COSTUME RENTAL HOUSES IN LOS ANGELES:

BILL HARGATE COSTUMES
1111 N. Formosa
Los Angeles, CA 90046
Phone: (213) 876-4432

COSTUME RENTAL CORP.
11149 Vanowen St.
N. Hollywood, CA 91605
Phone: (818) 753-3700

MOTION PICTURE COSTUME CO.
6844 Lankershim Blvd.
N. Hollywood, CA 91605
Phone: (818) 764-8191

PALACE COSTUME CO.
835 North Fairfax Ave.
Los Angeles, CA 90046
Phone: (213) 651-5458

REPEAT PERFORMANCE
318 North La Brea Ave.
Los Angeles, CA 90036
Phone: (213) 938-0609

THE HELEN LARSON COLLECTION
10415 Strong Ave.
Whittier, CA 90601
Phone: (310) 695-9992

UNITED-AMERICAN COSTUMES
12980 Raymer St.
N. Hollywood, CA 91605
Phone: (818) 764-2239

WESTERN COSTUME CO.   Phone: (818) 760-0900
11041 Vanowen St.
N. Hollywood, CA 91605

LEADING COSTUME HOUSES IN LONDON, ENGLAND:

ACADEMY COSTUMES LIMITED   Phone: 071-620-0771
50 Rushworth Street
London, SE1 0RB ENGLAND

ANGELS & BERMANS   Phone: 071-387-0999
40 Camden St.
London, NW1 9JR ENGLAND

COSPROP   Phone: 071-485-6731
26-28 Rochester Pl.
London, NW1 9JR ENGLAND

LEADING COSTUME HOUSES IN ROME, ITALY:

PERUZZI/COSTUMI D'ARTE   Phone: 06-511-5928
Piazzale A Tosti, #4
00147 Roma, ITALY

POMPEII   Phone: 39-6-487-4215
Via di S. Saba
00153 Roma, ITALY

TIRELLI COSTUMI   Phone: 39-6-321-2654
Via Pompeo Magno 11/B
00192 Roma, ITALY

LEADING COSTUME HOUSE IN VIENNA, AUSTRIA:

LAMBERT HOFER   Phone: 43-1-922-120
15, Hackengasse 10
1150 Wien, AUSTRIA

Following are some size conversion charts that may come in handy:

HATS

Measure in inches around the head. Military dress hats fit high on the head and are slightly smaller than civilian wear.

HAT SIZE	HAT SIZE EQUIVALENT	INCHES	DISTRIBUTION
XXS	$6^3/_8$	20 TO $20^1/_8$	1%
	$6^1/_2$	$20^1/_4$ TO $20^1/_2$	
XS	$6^5/_8$	$20^3/_4$ TO 21	4%
	$6^3/_4$	$21^1/_8$ TO $21^3/_8$	
S	$6^7/_8$	$21^1/_2$ TO $21^3/_4$	30%
	7	$21^7/_8$ v $22^1/_8$	
M	$7^1/_8$	$22^1/_4$ TO $22^1/_2$	44%
	$7^1/_4$	$22^5/_8$ TO $22^7/_8$	
L	$7^3/_8$	23 TO $23^1/_4$	18%
	$7^1/_2$	$23^3/_8$ TO $23^5/_8$	
XL	$7^5/_8$	$23^3/_4$ TO 24	2.5%
	$7^3/_4$	$24^1/_8$ TO $24^3/_8$	
XXL	$7^7/_8$	$24^1/_2$ TO $24^3/_4$	0.5%
	8	$24^7/_8$ TO $25^1/_8$	

GLOVES
To measure, put a measuring tape around the hand at the widest part, not including the thumb.

SIZE	SIZE EQUIVALENT	INCHES	MILITARY SIZE
S	7 TO 8	6½ TO 7	3
M	8½ TO 9½	7½ TO 8	4
L	10 TO 10½	8½ TO 9	5
XL	11	9½ TO 10	–

BOOTS AND SHOES
To convert from men's sizes to women's sizes, just take two sizes off the man's size (e.g., a man's 8 is a woman's 10).

INTERNATIONAL BOOT AND SHOE CONVERSATION CHART:

AMERICAN	6	7	8	9	10	11	12
BRITISH	5	6	7	8½	9	10	11
EUROPEAN	39	40	41	42	43	44	45
ASIAN	24½	25	26	27	28	29	30

MEN'S APPAREL

SUITS (NORMAL 6" DROP FROM CHEST TO WAIST — ATHLETIC CUT IS 8")

CHEST	36	40	42	44	46	48	50
WAIST	30	34	36	38	40	42	44
SIZE	S=34-36	M=38-40	L=42-44	XL=46-48	XXL=50	XXXL=52	

MEN'S SHIRTS:

NECK	13-13½	14-14½	15-15½	16-16½	17-17½	18-18½	19-19½
	XS	S	M	L	XL	XXL	XXXL

WOMEN'S APPAREL

SIZE	BUST	WAIST	HIP	SIZE EQUIVALENT
2	32	23	34	
4	33	24	35	XS
6	34	25	36	
8	35	26	37	S
10	36	27	38	
12	37½	28½	39½	M
14	39	30	41	
16	40½	31½	42½	L
18	42	33	44	
20	44	35	46	XL
22H	48	39	50	XXL
24H	50	41	52	
26H	52	43	54	
28H	54	45	56	

Collection of sketches and drawings.

1860
Study for bodice

155

1861
Concept, seated figure

1880 scout
Book illustration, "Indian scouts," John Langelier

1902 scout
Book illustration, "Indian scouts," John Langelier

Japanese pilot
Research sketch, *Pearl Harbor*

159

Mexican couple
Background types, *Geronimo*

Apache maid
Geronimo

Apache man
Geronimo

Arab man
Study for type, *The Wind and the Lion*

THE WIND AND THE LION
TEDDY ROOSVELT

Costume for Brian Keith
The Wind and the Lion

Costume for Roosevelt's wife
The Wind and the Lion

Asian girl
Concept, *Silent Flute*

Samurai
Concept, *Silent Flute*

Blues
Concept

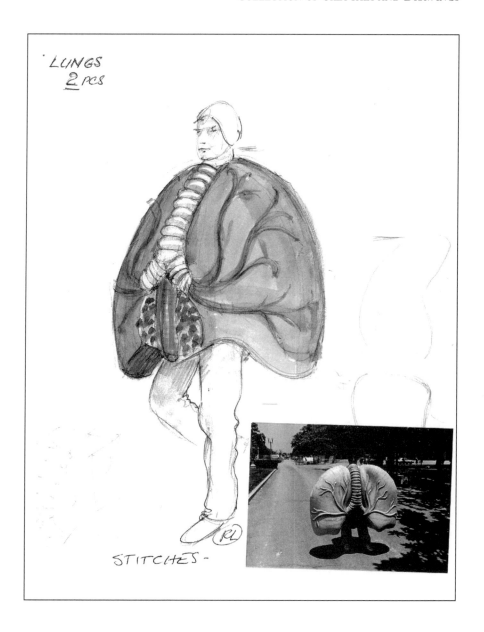

LUNGS
2 PCS

STITCHES –

"Lungs" walkaround
Stitches

Cowgirl
Concept, *Shaunessy*

Ranger
Sheriff, TV pilot, *Shaunessy*

Plains man
Crazy Horse

Plains woman
Crazy Horse

Dance couple
Concept, Disneyland

Western sketch
Saloon types, TV pilot, *Shaunessy*

ABOUT RICHARD LA MOTTE

Richard La Motte has worked in the television and film industries for thirty-five years, having organized and run costume departments in over seventeen states and seventeen foreign countries.

After graduating from high school, Richard joined the Marine Corps, where he illustrated classified briefings with a variety of visual arts including drawings, paintings, photography, and film.

In 1966, Richard became an entry-level costumer at Twentieth Century Fox. He rose through the ranks at Fox, working on such film hits as *Butch Cassidy and the Sundance Kid*, *Planet of the Apes*, and *M*A*S*H*, and such TV series as *Batman* and *Lost in Space*.

Mr. La Motte became the first minority and one of the first union members to cross over from Costumers Local #705 to the Costume Designers Guild when he gained his Costume Designer's card in 1974.

He designed costumes for such films as *The Wind and the Lion*, *A Man Called Horse II*, *The Island of Dr. Moreau*, *Rambo III*, *Goonies*, and was costume supervisor/costumer on *Reds, The Electric Horseman, Curse of the Pink Panther, Little Big Man, Dillinger*, and the upcoming *Gods and Generals*.

Richard has also been property master on *The Mask of Zorro*, military technical advisor on *The Last of the Mohicans*, and technical advisor on *Red Dawn* and *Pearl Harbor*.

Richard brings experience, wit, and wisdom to his valuable, detailed insider's view of both the art and business of costume design.

FROM WORD TO IMAGE
Storyboarding and the Filmmaking Process

Marcie Begleiter

Whether you're a director, screenwriter, producer, editor, or storyboard artist, the ability to tell stories with images is essential to your craft. This remarkable book is engineered to help both word- and image-oriented artists learn how to develop and sharpen their visual storytelling skills via story-boarding. Readers are taken on a step-by-step journey into the previsualization process, including breaking down the script, using overhead diagrams to block out shots, and creating usable drawings for film frames that collaborators can easily understand. Also includes discussions of compositional strategies, perspective, and figure notation as well as practical information on getting gigs, working on location, collaborating with other crew members, and much more.

Marcie Begleiter is a writer and educator who specializes in pre-visualization. She has worked extensively in the film, television, and interactive industries and is currently on the faculties of the Art Center College of Design and the American Film Institute.

$26.95
Order # 45RLS
ISBN: 0-941188-28-0

FILM & VIDEO BUDGETS
3rd Updated Edition

Deke Simon and Michael Wiese

For over 15 years *Film & Video Budgets* has been THE essential handbook for both beginning and professional filmmakers. Written by two pioneers of do-it-yourself film-making, this book outlines every element of production.

Updated and revised for digital video productions (and video-to-film transfers), this definitive book contains detailed formats and sample budgets for many different kinds of productions, from "no budget" digital movies to documentaries to a $5 million feature–along with all the crucial practical information that's made it an industry bible. Also includes new and highly useful materials, such as a comprehensive master list of line items for just about everything that could possibly be put into a production, and infor-mation-packed chapters on handling pre-production and setting up a pro-duction company. Also includes Excel sample budget templates down-loadable for free from the Web.

Deke Simon and Michael Wiese are veteran filmmakers who have had extensive experience in film, TV, and video.

$26.95
Order # 9RLS
ISBN: 0-941188-34-5

Budget samples include:
- $5 Million Feature Film
- Documentaries
  (both film and video)
- Industrial
- Music Video
- Student Film
- No-Budget Digital Feature
- Digital Video Feature
- Video-to-Film Transfer
- And more!

DIGITAL FILMMAKING 101
An Essential Guide to Producing Low-Budget Movies

Dale Newton and John Gaspard

The Butch Cassidy and the Sundance Kid of do-it-yourself filmmaking are back! Filmmakers Dale Newton and John Gaspard, co-authors of the classic how-to independent filmmaking manual *Persistence of Vision*, have updated their handbook for the digital age. *Digital Filmmaking 101* is your all-bases-covered guide to producing and shooting your own digital video films. It covers both technical and creative advice, from keys to writing a good script, to casting and location-securing, to lighting and low-budget visual effects. Also includes detailed information about how to shoot with digital cameras and how to use this new technology to your full advantage.

As indie veterans who have produced and directed three successful independent films, Gaspard and Newton are masters at achieving high-quality results for amazingly low production cost. They'll show you how to turn financial constraints into your creative advantage—and how to get the maximum mileage out of your production budget. You'll be amazed at the ways you can save money—and even get some things for free—without sacrificing any of your final product's quality.

Dale Newton and John Gaspard, who hail from Minneapolis, Minnesota, have produced three ultra-low-budget, feature-length movies and have lived to tell the tale.

$24.95
Order # 17RLS
ISBN: 0-941188-33-7

DIGITAL MOVIEMAKING

*A Butt-Kicking, Pixel-Twisting Vision
of the Digital Future and How to Make Your
Next Movie on Your Credit Card*

Scott Billups

You've got the script. You've got the vision. Now all you need is a deal to get your film made. But what if the powers-that-be say no? Do you have to give up your dream? Not any more. The digital revolution has made it cheaper and more possible than ever before for people to shoot and edit their own professional-quality films. This book will show you how to grab the bull by the horns and make your dream a reality.

Written for both experienced film and video directors who are new to the digital format and up-and-comers new to filmmaking in general, video guru Scott Billups' guide takes you through the brave new world of digital moviemaking. All the nuts-and-bolts information you need is right here, but technophobes need not fret. Billups explains in clear, concise, plain English what all these new terms and tools mean, and why it's not as hard as you think. He'll show you how to choose the technology that best fits your needs (and budget!) and how to get the maximum effect out of your equipment. Learn about different formats, effects tools, and cameras, as well as issues and challenges unique to shooting digitally.

Scott Billups has produced, directed, and written feature films, television programs, and commercials.

$26.95
Order # 2RLS
ISBN: 0-941188-30-2

INDEPENDENT FILM & VIDEOMAKER'S GUIDE
2nd Edition
Expanded & Updated

Michael Wiese

The new, completely expanded and revised edition of one of our best-sellers has all the information you need, from fundraising to distribution. This practical and comprehensive book will help filmmakers save time and money and inspire them to create successful projects.

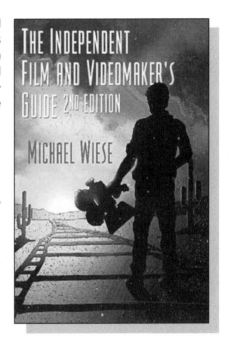

Contents include:

- Writing a business plan
- Developing your ideas into concepts, treatments, and scripts
- Directing, producing, and market research
- Understanding distribution markets (theatrical, home video, television, international)
- Financing your film
- Making presentations and writing a prospectus

Plus, an appendix filled with film cash flow projections, sample contracts, valuable contact addresses, and much more.

Using the principles outlined in this book, Wiese recently co-directed the short film *Field of Fish*, and is currently preparing his Bali feature. Additionally, Wiese is national spokesperson for Kodak's Emerging Filmmakers Program. He has conducted workshops on independent filmmaking in England, Germany, Finland, Indonesia, Ireland, Canada, Australia, and throughout the U.S. Contact Wiese at mw@mwp.com.

$29.95
Order # 37RLS
ISBN: 0-941188-57-4

FILM DIRECTING: SHOT BY SHOT
Visualizing from Concept to Screen

Steven D. Katz

This classic with the famous blue cover is one of the most well-known books in the business, and is a favorite of working directors as an on-set quick-reference guide. Packed with visual techniques for filmmakers and screenwriters to expand their stylistic knowledge, this international best-seller contains in-depth information on composition, previsualization, camera techniques, and much more. Includes over 750 storyboards and illustrations, with never-before-published storyboards from Spielberg's *Empire of the Sun*, Welles' *Citizen Kane*, and Hitchcock's *The Birds*.

$27.95
Order # 7RLS
ISBN: 0-941188-10-8

Both Katz Books Only $47

Save 12% when you order both books
Order #KatzB

....

FILM DIRECTING: CINEMATIC MOTION
A Workshop for Staging Scenes

Steven D. Katz

This follow-up to the phenomenally popular *Shot by Shot* is a practical guide to common production problems encountered when staging and blocking film scenes. Includes discussions of scheduling, staging without dialogue, sequence shots, actor and camera choreography, and much more. Also includes interviews with well-known professionals such as director John Sayles and visual effects coordinator Van Ling (*The Abyss, Terminator 2*).

$24.95
Order # 6RLS
ISBN: 0-941188-14-0

24 HOURS | 1.800.833.5738 | www.mwp.com

THE WRITER'S JOURNEY
2nd Edition
Mythic Structure for Writers

Christopher Vogler

See why this book has become an international best-seller and a true classic. First published in 1992, *The Writer's Journey* explores the powerful relationship between mythology and storytelling in a clear, concise style that's made it required reading for movie executives, screenwriters, scholars, and fans of pop culture all over the world.

Both fiction and nonfiction writers will discover a set of useful myth-inspired storytelling paradigms (i.e., "The Hero's Journey") and step-by-step guidelines to plot and character development. Based on the work of Joseph Campbell, *The Writer's Journey* is a must for all writers interested in further developing their craft.

The updated and revised 2nd Edition provides new insights, observations, and film references from Vogler's ongoing work on mythology's influence on stories, movies, and man himself.

Christopher Vogler, a top Hollywood story consultant and development executive, has worked on such high-grossing feature films as The Lion King *and* The Thin Red Line *and conducts writing workshops around the globe.*

$22.95
Order # 98RLS
ISBN: 0-941188-70-1

ORDER FORM

**TO ORDER THESE PRODUCTS, PLEASE CALL 24 HOURS - 7 DAYS A WEEK
CREDIT CARD ORDERS 1-800-833-5738 OR FAX YOUR ORDER (818) 986-3408
OR MAIL THIS ORDER FORM TO:**

MICHAEL WIESE PRODUCTIONS
11288 VENTURA BLVD., # 821
STUDIO CITY, CA 91604
E-MAIL: MWPSALES@MWP.COM
WEB SITE: WWW.MWP.COM

WRITE OR FAX FOR A FREE CATALOG

PLEASE SEND ME THE FOLLOWING BOOKS:

TITLE	ORDER NUMBER (#RLS _____)	AMOUNT
	SHIPPING	
	CALIFORNIA TAX (8.00%)	
	TOTAL ENCLOSED	

SHIPPING:
ALL ORDERS MUST BE PREPAID, UPS GROUND SERVICE ONE ITEM - $3.95
EACH ADDITIONAL ITEM ADD $2.00
EXPRESS - 3 BUSINESS DAYS ADD $12.00 PER ORDER
OVERSEAS
SURFACE - $15.00 EACH ITEM   AIRMAIL - $30.00 EACH ITEM

PLEASE MAKE CHECK OR MONEY ORDER PAYABLE TO:

MICHAEL WIESE PRODUCTIONS

(CHECK ONE) ____ MASTERCARD ____VISA ____AMEX

CREDIT CARD NUMBER _____

EXPIRATION DATE _____

CARDHOLDER'S NAME _____

CARDHOLDER'S SIGNATURE _____

SHIP TO:

NAME _____

ADDRESS _____

CITY _____ STATE _____ ZIP _____

COUNTRY _____ TELEPHONE _____

ORDER ONLINE FOR THE LOWEST PRICES

24 HOURS | 1.800.833.5738 | www.mwp.com